HOLINESS

Library of Congress Cataloging-in-Publication Data

Nicholl, Donald, 1923–1997
  Holiness / Donald Nicholl ; with a foreword by Ronald Rolheiser.—
3rd North American ed.
     p. cm.
  Includes index.
  ISBN 0-8198-3386-X (pbk.)
  1. Holiness. I. Title.
  BT767.N5 2005
  234'.8—dc22

                                        2004021753

Cover photo: Mary Emmanuel Alves, FSP

Interior photos: Mary Emmanuel Alves, FSP— pp. 8, 16, 46, 62, 74, 82, 96, 122, 138, 144, 152, 172, 184, 200, 210; Photodisc, Inc.— p. 32

Originally published by Darton, Longman and Todd, London, UK, 2004
First North American edition, New York: Seabury Press, 1981
Second North American edition, Mahwah, NJ: Paulist Press, 1987
Third North American editon, 2005

Published by Pauline Books & Media, 50 Saint Pauls Avenue, Boston, MA 02130-3491. Printed in U.S.A.

www.pauline.org

Pauline Books & Media is the publishing house of the Daughters of St. Paul, an international congregation of women religious serving the Church with the communications media.

1 2 3 4 5 6 7 8 9   11 10 09 08 07 06 05

HOLINESS

Donald Nicholl
With a foreword by Ronald Rolheiser

Pauline
BOOKS & MEDIA

Boston

Contents

Foreword

WE NEED A LANGUAGE FOR THE SOUL. ETERNAL TRUTHS MUST still find a vocabulary, so that they can be spoken and heard within a particular time and culture.

That's no easy thing. We've been trying to do this for years without much success. Often times a spiritual work, despite sound content, falls short, because its language is either too abstract or too pious, too much the technical talk of theologians, or the inner table talk of church circles.

When Henri Nouwen, perhaps the most successful spiritual writer of our generation, was writing, he worked long, and hard, and deliberately at his language. He used to rewrite his books many times over, trying to get just the right wording, searching always for a simpler way of saying things.

Eventually he developed a certain formula for writing spirituality. His carefully-honed recipe went something like this: He tried to be simple, without being simplistic; express deep sentiment, without being sentimental; be self-revealing, without being exhibitionistic; be deeply personal, yet profoundly universal; be explicitly Christian, without using the inner table talk of the worshiping community or the rote repetition of biblical language; be devotional, without being pious; speak from a clearly-committed stance, without being judgmental, exclusive, or doctrinaire; be contemporary, without being full of cliché and fad; be moral, without the alienating rhetoric of political correctness; speak always of God's invitation while respecting freedom and never proselytizing; be iconoclastic when necessary, yet always respecting where people are at; be both healthily deconstructionist and constructionist at the same time; use a language that radiates the joy of the resurrection, even as it leads deeper into the mystery of suffering, a language full of both hope and realism, energy and wisdom, a language deeply sensitive to human weakness, even as it challenges weakness and invites toward what is sublime, a language that's deeply compassionate, yet never compensatory.

That's quite a tightrope to walk. Yet that's precisely what Donald Nicholl does in this wonderful book on holiness. This is a work of disarming simplicity that is never simplistic. It recognizes and respects all the complexities, struggles, and rationalizations inside us, even as it challenges us, in a simple, clear language, to greater depth of soul. It's a deep book, deceptively so because of its simple language, that introduces its reader both to what's deep inside the wells of our ancient spiritual traditions and to what's deep inside the multiple crevasses layering his or her own heart.

You don't have to be a professional theologian or even a churchgoer to understand this book, though you will be equally challenged if you are. Its language and content transcend educational, religious, and denominational background.

This is a book for everyone, regardless of religious background or practice, beginner and proficient alike. It's for the enthused and the bitter, the committed and the indifferent, those inside our churches and those outside.

In the deep wells of our religious traditions there are some secrets worth knowing. This book, more often than not, will surprise you by showing you some of those secrets that you thought you knew but didn't.

RON ROLHEISER
Rome, Italy
May 25, 2004

Preface to the Second Edition

COMMON TO THE FOLK TRADITIONS OF ALL BRANCHES OF THE human family is a deep mistrust of the written word as a means of passing on their traditional wisdom. Many reasons are put forward in justification for this mistrust. For instance, those pious Jews known as Hasidim tried to prevent their teachings being written down on the grounds that once teachings are set down in black and white, then it becomes possible for anyone to read those words, even if they do so in a cold, sneering fashion, an attitude that in itself immediately inhibits the communication of wisdom.

Since I likewise recognize the limitations and the danger of the written word, it was only with great reluctance that I agreed to write a book on holiness. Now, however, I am glad that I did so, because the response of my readers has been anything but cold. Yet the very generosity of the readers' response to the book has made me all the more aware of a further limitation of the written word as opposed to face-to-face communication: with the written word one is not usually given a second chance that allows one to correct any mistaken impressions that might have arisen through one's unskilled writing.

Hence, I am doubly grateful to the publishers for affording me such a second chance with this new edition of *Holiness.*

There is one comment, in particular, that I wish to make in answer to a keen-eyed Australian correspondent. He wrote that an unwary reader of the book might easily gain the impression that anyone following the suggestions made in it will acquire holiness just as surely as a person who exercises with weights will acquire strong muscles. In order to prevent any such mistaken impression, therefore, let it be said at once that holiness is not a quality that we can set out to acquire like big muscles or a suntan. The truth is rather that we sometimes catch glimpses of holiness in the world about us, which make us aware of our own unholy condition and leave us longing to be at one with the Source of the holiness we have glimpsed, that is, the Holy One.

Such longing was memorably expressed by a man who was, indeed, crucified on account of it in the year 922. The man, Al-Hallaj, a Muslim mystic, once said that if he were to be given the choice of either joy or suffering from the hand of the Holy One, he would choose suffering—because then he could be sure that his longing was not for the gift but for the Giver. Though in the event, of course, Al-Hallaj discovered that a touch from the hand of the Holy One is always a touch of joy.

Holiness is a snare and a delusion unless it draws us into the Holy One.

DONALD NICHOLL

Acknowledgements

Thanks are due to the following for permission to quote from copyright sources:

Orbis Books: *The Gold-Crowned Jesus and Other Writings* by Kim Chi Ha;

The Editor of The Tablet: "Post Mortem" by Thomas Blackburn, from *The Tablet,* May 26, 1973;

Sri Rama Foundation: *Silence Speaks* by Baba Hari Dass.

I

Preliminaries

1

Teach Yourself?

A CERTAIN FEELING OF ABSURDITY COMES OVER ONE ON BEING asked to write a book about holiness, and then, in turn, to expect other people to read it after it has been written.

To begin with, one's immediate reaction must be much like that of Gandhi in the famous story told of him and a girl who was addicted to eating sweet foods. The story goes that a troubled mother one day came to Gandhi along with her daughter and explained to Gandhi that her daughter was in the habit of eating far more sweet food than was good for her. Please, she asked, would Gandhi speak to the girl and persuade her to give up this harmful habit? Gandhi sat for a while in silence and then said, "Bring your daughter back in three weeks' time, and then I will speak to her." The mother went away as she was told and came back after three weeks. This time Gandhi quietly took the daughter aside and in a few simple words pointed out to her the harmful effects of indulging in sweet food; he urged her to abandon the habit. Thanking Gandhi for giving her daughter such good advice, the mother then said to him in a puzzled voice, "Still, I would like to know, Gandhi-ji, why you did not just say those words to my daughter three weeks ago when I first brought her to you?" "But," explained Gandhi in reply, "three weeks ago I myself was still addicted to eating sweet foods!"

However, the sense of absurdity one feels in writing a book about holiness (or in reading one, if it comes to that!) does not arise simply out of a sense of one's own incompetence and unworthiness. It is rather that the enterprise itself borders on the comic. It reminds us of those pamphlets distributed in the thousands during the 1930s under the auspices of the Soviet government bearing the title, "Teach Yourself to be Godless." And it calls to mind those absurd systems of self-improvement which seem to consist in continually repeating to oneself, "Every day, in every way, I'm getting better and better," in the hope that much repetition of the words will eventually produce the desired result. What makes these examples absurd and comical is that godlessness and goodness are clearly qualities that cannot be produced by any kind of trick or technique as can, say, magic shows or computers.

Moreover, who wants to be caught red-handed reading a book entitled *How to Be Holy* or *Teach Yourself Holiness?* For if we are embarrassed when our friends discover that we are reading, say, about how to be better tennis players, or better lovers, or more successful after-dinner speakers, we are likely to be much more embarrassed when they discover that we are studying a book about how to be holy.

Of course, we can always try to escape from the embarrassment by adopting a detached attitude and saying that we are only doing so out of curiosity—because we are interested in comparing different attitudes toward the matter! Such a subterfuge is, in fact, the device adopted by many scholars who conceal their original interest in holiness by referring to it as an interest in comparative religion. And then later on these scholars discover that they have concealed their interest so thoroughly that they have now lost it.

The truth is that we have to cut through all this sense of incompetence, unworthiness, absurdity, comicality, and embarrassment by frankly and openly recognizing that we do read books on holiness in order to grow in holiness ourselves. Also, those who write books on holiness write them for exactly the same reason. The very act of trying to write about holiness is itself a search for holiness. It is not as though you first achieve holiness and afterward describe it, but, rather, that in trying to write about it the very process of writing serves as a kind of Geiger counter that discloses holiness to you. And even though that disclosure cannot simply be

> **The truth is that we have to cut through all this sense of incompetence, unworthiness, absurdity, comicality, and embarrassment by frankly and openly recognizing that we do read books on holiness in order to grow in holiness ourselves.**

reduced to a matter of technique, nevertheless there is a sense in which a few tips on the matter can be of great help.

In this respect the present book is, indeed, rather like such books as *Hints on Gardening* or *The Home Handyman;* just as those are not fundamental treatises on botany and architecture, so this book is not a fundamental treatise on holiness. For even as St. Paul in Athens was described by the philosophers as a "seed-picker," because he collected one scrap of knowledge here and another scrap of knowledge there, so it is with this book: it is a collection of scraps and hints and tips that have proved useful to a number of people and that might prove useful for the reader.

In other words, this is meant to be a really simple, practical book in the quite straightforward sense that as a result of it, so the author hopes, a number of people will grow in holiness—an area in which practice is everything and theory is nothing. I never saw this so clearly until the day when I read a statement by Philip Toynbee. Toynbee was reviewing a book about the future of England and comparing the present condition of the country to what it was like in the thirteenth century, when the Franciscan friars rejuvenated it. He said that what the country most needs now is an order of ecological friars who will go around the country similarly rejuvenating it.

"Okay, Philip," I said to myself, after reading his words, "off you go! If that is what the country most needs, you had better set off and *be* an ecological friar." One real, actual ecological friar is worth ten, twenty, even a million articles urging the existence of a whole order of ecological friars. Indeed, one real, existing ecological friar is worth more than a whole movement for the encouragement of ecological friars, with its many committees and a whole list of distinguished patrons.

The same is true of holiness: one truly holy person is worth more than any number of books about holiness. We need to bear this in mind particularly at the moment, when the market is being flooded with books on spirituality, meditation, mysticism, and so forth. Some people regard this flood as a sign that humanity is turning away from material things toward spiritual realities.

One truly holy person is worth more than any number of books about holiness.

That is certainly one possibility; but there is another possibility suggested by a group of editors of religious journals. When these editors were meeting recently, they discovered that the readership of all their journals was drawn almost entirely from the upper-income bracket of society; and a survey had shown their readers to have virtually no interest in articles about social justice, but a marked desire for articles about spirituality, mysticism, and holiness. This survey suggested to the editors in question that since their readers were already sufficiently affluent to be eating cake, they not only wanted the cake of affluence but they also desired on top of it the icing of spirituality and mysticism.

What the following pages have to offer is certainly not cake, much less icing, but just a few crumbs of dry bread that only become sweet if well chewed. Fortunately there are good precedents for collecting crumbs. When Jesus was

traveling in the region of Tyre and Sidon, a Canaanite woman asked him to heal her daughter, and Jesus replied that he had not been sent to Canaanites but to Israelites: "It is not fair to take the children's food and throw it to the house dogs." To which the Canaanite woman retorted, "Ah yes, sir; but even house dogs can eat the crumbs that fall from their master's table."[1] And Jesus himself later used a similar image when he said to the disciples after the miraculous feeding, "Pick up the crumbs that are left over, so that nothing gets wasted."[2]

By recycling the crumbs, Jesus gave an example for anyone who wants to grow in holiness. For many generations, thousands of the most gifted and exemplary human beings have been devoting all their energies of mind and body to becoming holy; on the way, they have let fall many crumbs of wisdom; it is a privilege, as well as a joy, to pick up those crumbs of wisdom and recycle them.

---

1. Mark 7:27–28.
2. John 6:12.

2

Knowledge of Holiness

—

ONE OF THE ASSUMPTIONS COMMONLY MADE THAT IS MOST likely to mislead a person is that knowledge of holiness is a form of knowledge just like every other form of knowledge, such as mathematics, physics, or geology. Not until we divest ourselves of this mistaken notion can we make any progress in our knowledge of holiness. For knowledge of this quality is found at the completely opposite end of the spectrum from, say, the science of mathematics.

The difference between these two extreme poles of the spectrum of knowledge becomes clear when we recognize, for instance, that the science of mathematics deals with the most abstract concepts of all: in pure mathematics, the concepts are totally unrelated to this concrete, material, living world in space and time. You could do pure mathematics even if no world existed, and even if you yourself did not exist except in an abstract form as pure mind. Moreover, even for us human beings as we do in fact exist at the moment, mathematics is abstract in the sense that the results of mathematical investigations do not essentially affect our lives in any way.

One can almost say the same of the form of knowledge next along the spectrum, that is, mathematical physics. But here there is a shift of attention, since it would not be possible to do mathematical physics if no world whatsoever existed. If this particular world of ours did not exist, this science could in fact be pursued, but it could not be pursued, it seems, if no world whatsoever existed. To that extent, mathematical physics is less abstract than pure mathematics itself.

Less abstract, again, than mathematical physics and so further along the spectrum of knowledge, comes the science of astronomy. For although astronomy is constantly having to posit abstract possibilities as a way of measuring time and space, nevertheless those possibilities have themselves to be measured against certain known quantities of this universe. It is true, of course, that astronomers are dependent upon their observational instruments in a way that mathematicians are not. And it is even true that the results of their science do remotely touch them personally, at least insofar as the question of the origin of the universe arises within their discipline. And insofar as the astronomer himself is part of the universe—though a peculiar part—the question of his own origin is bound to occur to his mind.

In this fashion, we can scan our way further along the whole spectrum of knowledge through the natural sciences and the social sciences until we come to that end of the spectrum where the study of man himself is located. A feature of this progression is that it steadily becomes less abstract, more and more related to this concrete, living world; and at every step the investigator is drawn ever more personally into this research.

The biologist's understanding of living beings, for instance, is achieved by means of concepts that are analogous to the language that is customarily used to express our experience as human beings, much more so than the concepts invoked by the astronomer or the mathematician. This is a reflection of the increased intimacy that the researcher feels toward living beings as contrasted with planets or the entities of mathematics.

How close that intimacy can be has been beautifully expressed by Roman Vishniac who believed that the science of life could not be taught by the use of dead organisms, and so developed a technique for photographing microscopic creatures alive and in their free-swimming state. Vishniac tells us:

> I was watching a mosquito's head one night under 200-power magnification and I was astounded by the loveliness of the eyes. Every one of the compound facets was burning in a wonderful color like gold falling from a setting sun onto the windows of a castle in fairyland. It was so beautiful that I loved this mosquito. But I watched too long. I had no water cell before the lamp, and I didn't realize the strength of the light. Suddenly it was killing him. One by one the colors of his eyes went out like lights being turned off back of the windows, and through the microscope.
>
> I saw the death of this mosquito. And I can tell you it is such a terrible thing—death.[3]

---

3. Roman Vishniac, *Creativity: The Human Resource.* Brochure for an exhibition held at San Francisco, 1979.

Such intimacy increases steadily as we move along the spectrum: in the eyes of students of literature, for instance, humankind is more complex and concrete than either the economic man or political man known to the social sciences. Unlike the economic or political scientist—and still more unlike the mathematician or astronomer—the student of literature becomes uncomfortably aware that there is no possibility of standing off remote from the object of one's research. If, for instance, one is writing about Dostoyevsky, the awareness that this man Dostoyevsky "knew more about human psychology than all the members of the International Psychoanalytical Association put together" can hardly be avoided. As a consequence of Dostoyevsky's knowledge of human psychology, whenever the literary researcher gazes into the world of Dostoyevsky, he suddenly discovers himself being scrutinized by a pair of terrifyingly penetrating eyes: the researcher has now become the object of the research!

Located at that end of the spectrum, knowledge of holiness exemplifies the trend we have traced in its ultimate, pure form. Here, at the opposite pole from pure mathematics, knowledge of holiness is not concerned with abstract concepts which are totally unrelated to this concrete, material, living world in space and time and which do not affect our lives in any essential way. On the contrary, it is concerned with concrete reality, with how persons assume total responsibility for the material, living world in which they find themselves at a particular place and a particular time.

Moreover, the object of our research, holiness (whether of human beings or of God), turns the tables on us, so to speak. When we try to look into the eyes of the Buddha, say, or of St. Francis, we soon find that their eyes are, in their turn, gazing into ours, scrutinizing us, burning out the impurity behind our motives for looking into their lives.

> **When we try to look into the eyes of the Buddha, say, or of St. Francis, we soon find that their eyes are, in their turn, gazing into ours, scrutinizing us, burning out the impurity behind our motives for looking into their lives.**

This turning of the tables is frightening, and it is obviously one of the reasons why many people refuse to pay much attention to holiness. When you had been thinking you were the hunter, it is frightening suddenly to discover that all the time you have actually been the hunted one. You imagined that you had taken the initiative in pursuit of the Holy One, and then realize that in truth it was the Holy One who initiated the pursuit.

Terribilis est locus iste, "This is a terrifying place," declared Jacob when he awoke at Bethel. "This is the house of God; this is the gate of heaven."[4] Yet Jacob had been attracted to that very spot; he had been drawn to it, fascinated by the dream of holy angels. The Holy One is both attractive and terrifying: "It is a dreadful thing to fall into the hands of the living God,"[5] we are told in the Letter to

---

4. Genesis 28:11–17.
5. Hebrews 10:31.

the Hebrews; though it would be more dreadful to fall out of them.

Therefore, in some ways, one feels it would be better never to have any contact with holiness of any kind. Certainly it would be more comfortable because the demands made upon us, if we are to acquire knowledge of holiness, are terrifying. The trouble is that once you find yourself launched upon the road to holiness there is no turning back, ever. Your best chance really is to make sure that you never actually leave base, but seek assurance instead by repeating to yourself that the aspiration toward holiness is a vain illusion; sanctity is an impossible ideal, unattainable by frail human beings. This is a stance which can be maintained so long as you take care never to meet a holy person, whether in the flesh or on

> **The trouble is that once you find yourself launched upon the road to holiness there is no turning back, ever.**

film or in a book—but especially in the flesh, because if you had met, say, Mother Teresa, you could no longer go on saying that sanctity is all very well in theory, but in fact it is impossible. It has been done; therefore it can be done; and excuses are no longer plausible. For this reason, shrewd, worldly people give holy people a wide berth, keeping their distance from them, knowing in their shrewd, worldly way that holy people are dangerous; they are dynamite.

Many thinkers in the past have recognized that these features peculiar to knowledge of holiness require us to

give it a special name to distinguish it from the natural knowledge such as one acquires through studying mathematics, physics, geology, and so forth. They have called it connatural knowledge since the word "connatural," at its root, means "in accordance with nature"—so that there is an accordance between the nature of the person knowing and the nature of the object known.

To give an example: in order to know what purity is, the natural thing to do is to look up the definition of purity in a dictionary, because the dictionary is a source of natural knowledge. But another way would be to consult a pure person, someone whose knowledge of it springs from their own nature; the knowledge, then, is in accordance with this nature and so is entitled connatural knowledge. This second way of inquiry would likely lead the inquirer further to allow his or her own nature to be purified, in accordance with purity itself, and thus the inquirer would also have acquired a connatural knowledge of purity. His or her own nature would then be a source of connatural knowledge.

In natural knowledge, knowing and being can be separate—a lepidopterist does not need to be a butterfly. But with connatural knowledge, to know and to be cannot be separate; they are two aspects of the one act. To know what purity is you have to be pure. To know what holiness is you have to be holy.

Of course there are degrees of knowledge; a person can have some inkling of what holiness is without being completely holy. Nevertheless, by degrees one either ascends or descends; and unless a person is ascending by degrees toward complete holiness, being changed at every step, that person cannot be said to be truly studying holiness. In fact, one can affirm quite confidently that if a person claims to have studied holiness, but has not been changed in the course of doing so, then it was not holiness that he was studying but something else. As the saying goes, "The Holy One is the One whom one can never search for in vain."

Not that the process of change is in any sense mechanical or excludes the possibility of tragic failure. There are only too many examples of such tragedies in the human story. A particularly painful one in recent years was the case of the brilliant German thinker Max Scheler. A professor at Munich University, of Jewish ancestry, Scheler was converted to the Catholic faith at the age of 42. From that time onward he devoted more and more of his lectures to expounding the meaning of sanctity and to writing about such figures as St. Benedict, Dante, and St. Francis. The fruit of these years of study is to be found in the book that Scheler published in 1922, *On the Eternal in Man,* a book that was received with great acclaim.

But in the meantime, there had begun to develop in Scheler's person a split between his knowledge and his being. At the same time that he was expounding the sanctity of St. Francis or St. Benedict in his lectures and writings, his personal life was becoming more and more disordered and chaotic. For a time he was able to hold together this contradiction between knowing and being, but eventually something had to snap, as was gently pointed out to Scheler at this period by the Archbishop of Cologne. There is something pathetically misguided in Scheler's reply to the Archbishop: "I only point the way; a sign does not have to go where it points."[6] For the truth is that in the field of connatural truths a sign eventually does have to go where it points, otherwise it finds itself pointing in the wrong direction.

That is precisely what happened to Scheler when he published his last major book, *The Position of Man in the Cosmos*, a confused work in which his earlier aspirations are thwarted by his sense of the "impotence of the Spirit." As he wrote to his ex-wife on May 10, 1926, "I live in loneliness, buried in ice."[7]

The tragic story of Scheler is a sharp lesson to us all that it is no light matter to undertake the study of holiness. There is no way of knowing about holiness that does not involve one in actually knowing holiness, coming to grips with it in the same way that Jacob at Peniel came to grips with the angel.[8] And just as Jacob, after that night of struggle, was left with his hip dislocated, so anyone wrestling with holiness is likely to find his secure, comfortable existence put out of joint. Before he arrived at Peniel (which means "I have seen God") the son of Isaac was called "the supplanter" (i.e. Jacob), but after being touched by the Holy One he was changed into "the preserver with God" (i.e. Israel). You cannot approach holiness without being changed into either a supplanter or a preserver.

6. J. R. Staude, *Max Scheler* (New York, 1967), p. 254.
7. J. M. Oesterreicher, *Walls are Crumbling* (London, 1953), p. 173.
8. Genesis 32:24.

Diagram A   *Diagram B*

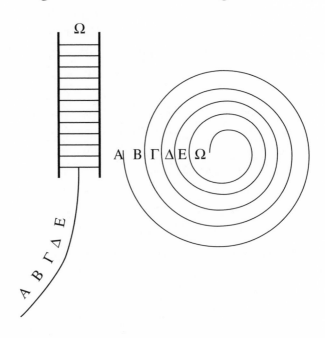

A = The first moment of creation
B = The formation of the earth
Γ = The appearance of life
Δ = The beginning of consciousness
E = Self-consciousness
Ω = Self-sacrifice

Note on Diagram A

In no time the universe came into being; and then there was time. Being and time are concomitant. But time has a different quality, a different intensity, according to the kind of being with which it is concomitant. Starting from point Alpha the quality of being, and therefore of time, intensi-

fies as inert matter is transcended by life, and life by consciousness, and so forth with intensifying steepness until
the climax is achieved (Omega) through a self-conscious
being who sacrifices himself for the sake of others. No
being, neither man nor God, can go any further; there is no
further to go. That is the end of time. Once more, as in the
beginning, it is no time, because both being and time have
now been totally transcended; they are fulfilled.

Once the complete act of self-sacrifice has been
achieved, then the quality of being, and of time, is changed
for all beings. So no matter what the quantity of their lives
may be, as measured by the chronological time of inert matter, nevertheless the quality of the time in which they live
is end-time. Traditionally this has been called eternal life.

On our diagram the horizontal line from Alpha, representing chronological time, transcends into the vertical line
of Jacob's Ladder. The line of that ladder upon which the
angels ascend and descend is the very same line as that
upon which the angels bear every sacrifice of self no matter at what point on the horizontal line, in chronological
time, the sacrifice may take place.

It will also be seen that what we, as creatures on the
lower side of the curving line, take to be acts of gradual
transcendence are really, when seen from the higher side of
the line, in eternal light, one act of creation that takes no
time.

3

Our Place in Creation

WHAT SCHELER SAID ABOUT MAN IN *THE POSITION OF MAN IN THE COSMOS* may well have been misguided, but at least he did recognize that there is an intimate connection between the picture that human beings hold of their position in the cosmos and the sort of wholeness and holiness that they regard as feasible for human beings. If there is no such harmonious connection between a person's image of his own position and his image of the cosmos in which he lives—but, on the contrary—a jarring discord between them, then all his efforts to achieve wholeness and holiness will be frustrated from the beginning. It will be like trying to run with a heavy ball of doubt attached to one leg.

That is why a phrase often used to commend simple faith is so misguided. It is said, for instance, in commendation of the famous scientist Louis Pasteur, that in spite of his great scientific knowledge, "he had the faith of a Breton peasant." While it is all very well for a Breton peasant to have the

faith of a Breton peasant, it is not really praiseworthy for a
modern scientist to hold the faith in the same manner.
Modern science opens vistas before us upon the origin and
age of the universe, of our earth and of human beings, upon
genetics, psychology, comparative religion, and scriptural
teaching that are quite incompatible with the image of the
cosmos traditional among the Breton peasantry.

To try to close one's eyes to these vistas is dishonest
and, therefore, self-defeating. But equally it betokens
ingratitude of heart and pettiness of spirit that lead one to
despise the richness and the mysteries of creation. The discovery of ever-deeper mysteries and ever-more abundant
riches should constitute an invitation to grow more wholesome and open-hearted in one's spiritual life. To refuse that
invitation means ultimately to stunt and deaden that life.

For the whole of creation is our guru, our teacher; we
have no need to be afraid of our teacher. When Pascal, gazing at the starry heavens, said, *"Le silence de ces espaces
infinies m'éffrait"* ("The silence of this infinite space makes
me afraid"), he was in a manner expressing fear before his
guru, his teacher, and turning his back on him. And why
he did so is instructive for us. He had lost the sense, which
the Psalmist enjoyed, in common with most of humanity
until Pascal's day, of how the starry heavens declare the
glory of the Lord, a declaration that can be heard in the
music of the planets if only we have ears to hear.

Before Pascal's generation, human beings heard that
music; indeed, the teaching of astronomy in the medieval
universities began with a course on music, so vital was the
connection in their minds between all the harmonies of

creation, between the song of praise sung by sun and moon and stars, ice and snow, and sea beasts and birds of heaven. Above all, there was a connection between the outer world of the heavens and the inner world of man because, as Dante said, it is the same Love that moves our hearts as moves the sun and the other stars.

What is so instructive about Pascal's case is that the silence which science seemed to have decreed for the heavens in his generation, and which seemed to cast a deathly fear upon humankind, is now recognized by science itself to be full of an infinite variety of harmonies. The story of how this new thinking has come about illustrates how, time and again, a scientific discovery that seems at first to rob the universe of some of its richness later on proves to offer an even deeper sense of wonder and mystery. It is only a question of waiting, of not being frightened of one's guru, of patiently trusting that reality can never let one down. For the image offered to us by modern science is of a cosmos which is pulsating and vibrating at every level, on an infinite variety of scales, from the tiniest neuron which vibrates at a rate of millionths of a second to the universe itself, whose expansion and contraction are themselves to be perceived as a vibration on the scale of millions of light years.

In recent times, certain spiritual masters have discovered all over again how to hear this music of creation in our immediate surroundings. For instance, the recently canonized Greek saint, Nectarius, was able to teach a whole community of nuns on the island of Egina to hear the song sung by the trees. Not far away from Egina, moreover, lived Father Joseph, the most skillful grafter of trees, who attributed his grafting skill to his ability to distinguish between the songs of the different saplings and trees; this enabled him to tell which graft would harmonize with the main stem. Father Joseph maintained that anyone who listened carefully enough could hear the vibrations of the sap circulating in the tree.

After all, a mere 200 years ago it would have seemed impossible that such a simple instrument as a radio receiver on one side of the earth could one day pick up the music being played some 12,000 miles away on the other side of the earth. And yet that "impossibility" goes on all the time now and never causes so much as a raised eyebrow, which surely makes it comparatively easy for us to realize that when we human beings are properly attuned, we can indeed hear the music of the spheres and be inspired by it. The silence which Pascal feared has since proved to be our guru, drawing us into ever more wonderful music.

And yet it remains true that few people seem to have drawn out from the vistas opened up by natural science the sort of lessons for spirituality that are contained there. Usually we behave as though our spiritual lives are almost a foreign element incongruously inserted into a universe that is neutral, totally indifferent toward our aspirations, whereas the new vistas actually reveal to us that we human beings represent the point of all this whirling creation insofar as we are seeking holiness. Holiness is not an optional extra to the process of creation but rather the whole point of it.

> **Holiness is not an optional extra to the process of creation but rather the whole point of it.**

This principle becomes clear if we let our minds range over the story of creation as we can now envisage it. For apparently it is truly a creation in the sense that there was a beginning and that something totally new appeared: our universe. In no time our universe in time began, something totally new.

According to some estimates, that event took place some 20,000 million years ago. If we represent the time span since that event by means of a straight line, the line being some seven inches long, the line representing the formation of the earth upon which we live would be one inch long, since our earth was formed some 3,400 million years ago.

The next point at which newness entered into creation was at the moment when life appeared, whether the life on our earth or in some sphere of the universe as yet unknown to us. That was, comparatively speaking, a recent event; so, if we continue to represent the time dimension of the universe in a linear fashion, this transcendence of previous conditions which we call life has to be represented by a steep upward curve (see diagram A, p. 20). The line then curves upward even more sharply at the next new manifestation, which is consciousness such as we find in higher forms of life. This itself is followed by a further act of transcendence when a new reality appears; that is, self-consciousness in a creature conscious of being a self among other selves. Man, of course, is such a creature.

Finally the line steepens so sharply as to become vertical; in that sense the line of time has come to the end. A totally new reality is enacted, one which transcends all circumstances of time, yet which itself gives point to the whole line of time. This new reality is the act of self-sacrifice deliberately carried out on behalf of others by a self-conscious being. Neither man nor God can go any further than that: there is no further to go; it is the ultimate. Nothing in the whole process of the creation throughout the 20,000 million years since the beginning could have prepared one for such transcendence. No one who was not already aware from beyond the process of the reality of self-sacrifice could have predicted it from the process. It is beyond the process because it is what gives point to the process (diagram B, p. 20).

The most memorable instance of such perfect self-sacrifice is that of Jesus when he offered himself at Golgotha on behalf of the whole of creation. But there are many other instances throughout the ages, and even in our own day we have witnessed them. To take only one example, we can quote the deeds of Father Maximilian Kolbe during the Second World War. This Polish priest, in a concentration camp, voluntarily sacrificed his own life by offering to take the place of one of his fellow prisoners who had been chosen for execution.

Islam expresses most beautifully the truth that in man we have been brought to the ultimate point of creation when it says:

> Man is the seal of the degree of creation, for after him no species has come into existence and he is the sealing of the hand of Omnipotence...he is the divine seal which has been put on the page of contingency.[9]

9. A. Schimmel, *Pain and Grace* (Leiden, 1976), p. 77.

Earlier, St. Paul had coined an unforgettable image for
this achievement when he wrote in his Letter to the
Ephesians that God "has let us know the mystery of his
purpose, the hidden plan he so kindly made in Christ from
the beginning, to act upon when the times had run their
course to the end: that he would bring everything together
under Christ, as head, everything in the heavens and everything on earth."[10]

Actually, the original Greek words that St. Paul
wrote are much more powerful than this English translation, especially the word *anakephalaiosasthai,* of
which the root *kephalos* means "head," so that it may be
better to translate the phrase: "God recapitulated in
Christ all the rich possibilities of creation, both those on
earth and those in heaven." By recapitulating all, by
standing at the head of all, Christ acted as the representative of creation. And only that one who is prepared to
sacrifice his part can act as the representative for the
whole (for others); a part has to cease to be apart if it is
to encompass the whole.

For anyone seeking wholeness and holiness this truth
has many implications. To begin with, it makes one realize that each human being constitutes a recapitulation,
an "en-heading" of creation, because each one of us is
heir to the whole struggle that has gone on over endless
eons to achieve transcendence. And we humans are the
creatures who have been brought to that culminating
point of final transcendence at which we are called to

10. Ephesians 1:9–10.

self-sacrifice. As St. Paul says, "From the beginning until now the entire creation has been groaning in one great act of giving birth."[11]

The most appropriate word to describe this act is the word *agonia,* a Greek word that connotes both struggle and anguish. No other word so well describes Jesus' act of self-sacrifice through the struggle he had with himself, his agony in the garden of Gethsemane. His was an agony that gave meaning to all the previous agony of creatures throughout the ages, throwing light back upon the apparent meaninglessness of all preceding struggles, thereby redeeming them.

Wonderfully, one is sometimes granted a vivid glimpse into those preceding eons. To me that happened one spring morning when I set out at dawn and walked from the top of the Grand Canyon down the steep path that leads to the bottom where the Colorado river flows, some 7,000 feet below. As you descend the Canyon you can observe on its walls layer upon layer of the sediments that have formed over millions of years, and you can relate those layers to the successive species of living creatures, both fauna and flora, that dwelt upon this earth before we appeared: Permian ferns and crinoids and armor-plated fish.

Observing traces of them in this way, you feel a true kinship with all those beings, knowing that both they and you trace your existence back to that first moment of transcendence when life appeared on this earth. And then you start to reflect that the very eyes with which you are

---

11. Romans 8:22.

observing these wondrous evidences are themselves the
result of millions of years of striving for light, ever since the
first pin-hole eye appeared on those primitive marine creatures, the cephalopods. And you are the beneficiary of all
that struggle for light, the heir to all that agony.

As you gaze at your hands or think of your ears or of
your tongue it takes your breath away to envisage the innumerable strivings that had to be
attempted before you could see
and touch and hear and taste and
speak. Had any breakdown in that
series of stirrings occurred it could
have destroyed the possibility for
you to see and hear and sing. The
breakdown was prevented by
untiring faithfulness on the part of
millions of beings. The mere
thought of this makes you realize
what an incredibly hard-won privilege it is simply to be a human
being; and at the same time it is an awesome responsibility.
Every human being has a responsibility toward all those
creatures whose agony and groaning has given us birth.

> Every human being
> has a responsibility
> toward all those
> creatures whose
> agony and groaning
> has given us birth.

This sense of responsibility is the answer to that feeling
of meaninglessness that overcame Pascal in the face of the
silence of the heavens and has afflicted many millions of
people since. These latter formulate their feelings of
insignificance by saying that science has demonstrated that
humanity is not the center of the universe: Galileo showed
that the earth is not the center of our solar system, but sim-

ply one of many planets that circle around the sun; Darwin showed that we are not a special creation, but simply the product of natural selection, like all other forms of life; and Freud showed that our lofty spiritual ideals are simply a reflection of sexual instincts.

But, as we have indicated in the previous pages, such a view of our position in the universe is not the only one— nor, indeed, the most probable when we also take into account that revelation of what it means to be a human being which we receive when we open our eyes to the witness of self-sacrifice. Self-sacrifice is an act of total responsibility whereby we take complete hold of ourselves and place ourselves at the disposition of the whole; we cease to be apart and become one with the whole. We then "re-present" the whole.

If we continue to think in terms of our diagram (B) we realize that a point within a circle (our self within the universe) cannot encompass the whole of the circle so long as that point is off-center; its compass line will include some of the circle for a certain distance, but will miss out other parts and occasionally even go outside the circle altogether. It is only by concentrating ourselves, distilling the inmost meaning of ourselves through taking complete responsibility for ourselves, that we can become the point at the absolute center of the circle which encompasses the whole of the circle.

And then we have to remember that the crucial characteristic of a point is that it does not occupy space. So that anyone longing to find themselves at the absolute center has to contract and contract until they finally reach the

vanishing point. It is only when we vanish that the point of our lives is revealed, when we sacrifice our selves completely. If we do not eventually manage that, then we leave behind a confused blur that seems to have no point. By self-sacrifice the point becomes crystal-clear.

Two memorable illustrations, one from the cosmos and one from human culture, enable us to hold this truth vividly in our minds.

For the cosmic illustration we turn to the black holes spoken of by modern astronomers. According to these astronomers a whole universe may suddenly start to contract. As it does so, its density increases, and this in its turn accelerates even further the rate of its contraction. Eventually this increasing density produces such a curvature of matter that the universe passes beyond perception, leaving a black hole. According to certain theories, this universe may then reappear in some distant realm of reality.

Strangely similar to this cosmic vision of black holes is the illustration from human culture that is provided in the book *Born in Tibet*, by Chögyam Trungpa. There we learn of a very saintly man in northeast Tibet whose compassion was so great that he always helped everyone in need and opened his house at all times to pilgrims and the very poor. When this old man was approaching death he said: "When I die you must not move my body for a week; this is all that I desire."

Soon he did die and his body, wrapped in old clothes, was carried into a small room. The corpse-bearers noted that though the old man had been tall, the body already appeared to have grown smaller. On the sixth day, when the family peered into the room, they saw that it had grown still smaller. On the eighth day, however, when the men came to bear the body to the cemetery and they undid the coverings, there was nothing inside except nails and hair. Everyone, of course, was astounded. But when the family reported the event to a learned local lama, the learned man told them that a similar happening had been reported several times in the past: the body of the saintly man had been absorbed into the Light.[12]

The culminating point of all creation is self-sacrifice.

A whole universe vanishes. The body of a saintly man vanishes. With these two illustrations we are made aware of the parallels between the course of events in the visible cosmos and the course of events in our spiritual life. That course is the way of contraction, of concentration to the point at which one vanishes. The culminating point of all creation is self-sacrifice.

---

12. Chögyam Trungpa, *Born in Tibet* (London, 1966), p. 96.

II

~

Practice

4

Beginning

⚊

THE MOST DIFFICULT TASK IS TO BEGIN. WE ARE ALL AWARE OF this, whether the task is getting out of bed in the morning or starting to write a long-overdue letter. Since this matter of holiness is essentially paradoxical, it is true that beginning in holiness is also quite simple because we can begin at any time and at any place. In that sense it is not like gardening, say, when you have to collect spades and forks before you can begin; here you need no special tools nor special preparation, nothing but the desire to get on with the job. In fact, anyone who has stayed with this book so far has already begun—though maybe not yet in a very conscious or resolute fashion.

The simplicity of these early stages is well expressed in the Indian saying that "if you take one step toward God, then God will take ten steps toward you." Of course, you have actually to take the step; it is no good bargaining with God and saying, "Very well, then: if I do this one thing for you, tell me the ten things you will do for me." Talking like that is not taking any step whatsoever; it is simply finding a reason for not taking a step under the cover of bargaining.

And once you start bargaining, that is all you are ever likely to do—until you stop bargaining. Gandhi showed himself well aware of our human capacity for deceiving ourselves in that fashion when he said, "If you don't find God in the very next person you meet, it is a waste of time looking for him further." Gandhi knew that we all try to get out of finding God by saying to ourselves, "No, not in this person but in another more suitable one further along the line." In a similar fashion, people often say, "I will give up smoking as soon as I have finished this next packet of cigarettes," though everybody knows that it is perfectly simple to give up smoking: don't smoke the next cigarette, and then all the other cigarettes will take care of themselves.

We see that Gandhi enjoyed that priceless gift of holy teachers: the ability to shake people into beginning their spiritual work. He did this by means of short, unforgettable sayings. Another such teacher was Rabi'a, the woman Muslim mystic who lived in Baghdad 1,000 years ago. On one occasion some of her followers asked her to describe to them the first step you have to take in order to achieve the virtue of patience. Rabi'a simply replied, "Stop complaining."

At first, her followers were disappointed not to hear some more elevated and elevating discourse, something more spiritual. But eventually the impact of Rabi'a's blow struck them. It continued ringing in their skulls, so that whenever the impulse to complain arose within them, they would hear Rabi'a's voice saying, "stop complaining"; and they knew that until they stopped complaining, it was a waste of time to talk about patience.[13] All they needed to do was to stop the next time they felt an impulse to complain.

Rabi'a's words remind us of the words spoken by Father Zossima to Fyodor Karamazov when the latter was indulging in his usual play acting as a way of deceiving both himself and others. Zossima simply said: "Don't lie."[14] He did not treat Fyodor to a homily on honesty—about the meaning of which we may quibble. He just told him to stop lying, the meaning of which we all know beyond a doubt.

It is beyond doubt that the call to start on the way of holiness is quite simple.

It is also beyond doubt that the call to start on the way of holiness is quite simple. Sometimes what we are required to do may seem humdrum and sometimes it seems dramatic; but in either case it is simple. What could be more humdrum, for instance, than the advice given by the Vietnamese Buddhist priest, Thich Nhat Hanh, to someone seeking a spiritual way? To start with, he says, draw your lips into a faint, scarcely perceptible smile.

That may seem a small thing, but in fact it makes a big difference; for once we do what Thich Nhat Hanh suggests, most of us discover, to our surprise, that we are in the habit

---

13. Margaret Smith, *Rabi'a the Mystic* (San Francisco, 1977), pp. 61–2.

14. F. M. Dostoyevsky, *The Brothers Karamazov*, bk. 1, ch. 2.

of frowning. By altering that ingrained habit we are ready
to greet our fellow human beings with a smile. Until we can
accomplish such small acts as a beginning, it is vanity to
seek for more heroic tasks.

Another incident concerning Thich Nhat Hanh under-
lines this truth. At the height of the conflict in Vietnam he
was much in demand as a speaker on the university cam-
puses of the United States. On one occasion, having given
a lecture, he was questioned by a student who had been
caught up into fashionable techniques of meditation. The
student said to him, "Could you tell us how you meditate in
your monastery in Vietnam?" To this Thich Nhat Hanh
replied, "In our monastery no one is allowed to meditate
until he has spent at least three years learning how to serve
tea to the older monks."

But if the humdrum task of serving tea to the older
monks may be the beginning for many, nevertheless others
may be called in a more dramatic way. For instance, there
was a man lying desperately ill in the hospital, almost out
of his mind with terror and confusion induced by the drugs
administered to him. Nothing of his true self seemed to
remain except a tiny particle the size of a grain of mustard
seed. Outside that particle all was chaos and darkness.

Suddenly he heard a voice from the nearby corridor:
"I'm that bloody lonely I could cry." It was the voice of an
old miner who was in the hospital for the first time in his
life, and had been left for a while in a wheelchair in the corridor. The old miner had cried out because he was overwhelmed by the impersonality of it all. Hearing the terror
in the old man's voice, the desperately ill man in the

neighboring ward, from the pit of his own terror, said to himself: "I'll go out and sit by him if it's the last thing I do."

And so he did. And from that moment his own terror began to lift. A process of healing had begun in him, so that soon he was more whole than ever before in his life. In the voice of the old man he had heard the voice of God calling him to wholeness and holiness. You can begin anytime, anywhere, even if you are only a tiny grain of mustard seed lying in a pit of terror.

In fact, it is often through realizing that for each of us there will be a "last thing that I do" that we are spurred on to take the first step on the road to holiness. Naturally this realization occurs frequently late in life when people become aware of approaching the last thing they are going to do. For instance, when he was in his nineties, the skeptical agnostic Bertrand Russell, remembering the vision of his youth, wrote, "The loneliness of the human soul is unendurable; nothing can penetrate it except the highest intensity of the sort of love that religious teachers have preached; whatever does not spring from this motive is harmful, or at least useless."[15]

In those words of Russell, we can hear an echo of that same longing which inspired St. John of the Cross to say, "In the evening of our lives we shall be examined in love," or which inspired Léon Bloy to write that haunting sentence, "There is only one sadness, the sadness of not being a saint." The sentence is a haunting one, because ordinarily we allow ourselves to be saddened by failures of every kind: the failure

---

15. Bertrand Russell, *Autobiography* vol. I, (London, 1967), p. 146.

to become as famous as we had once dreamed of being, the failure to be rich, or beautiful, or a model of health.

All these failures, and endless others, are constant and nagging sources of sadness to us throughout our lives. But when we reach the end of our lives, we shall realize that none of these things that have caused us so much heartache are really cause for ultimate sadness—none of them matters any longer. The only sadness, now, is the sadness of not being a saint.

In no tradition is this awareness of last things more intensely nurtured than in Tibetan Buddhism. Tibetan Buddhists often show astonishment when they come to discover how rarely and irresolutely Westerners, even educated Westerners, meditate upon the fact of death. To them it is amazing that anyone with any claim to enlightenment, or desire for it, should not meditate very realistically, with the utmost concentration, upon the one undeniable certainty about our lives, which is that each of our lives will be ended by death.

Until we have in some measure integrated this certainty into our very being, we shall continue to exist in a state of confusion, pulled one way by one desire and the opposite way by another. Whereas, if we constantly remember death, we begin to see life with extraordinary clarity; the desires and attachments that have been obscuring our vision disperse like clouds before the great sun of death, and the shape of our lives becomes crystal clear.

Above all, the effect of this sharp light is to reveal to us everything that we shall have to let go of at death; in doing so, moreover, it reveals to us the unsuspected depths of our attachments—to property, health, learning, the esteem of others, and so on. Conversely, it shows us that absolutely nothing of all these attachments belongs to us; they are all on temporary loan.

Once we realize that we own absolutely nothing, we are enlightened, not only in the sense that our minds are flooded with light, but also in the sense that a weight is lifted from us and our hearts grow lighter. Which is not to say, of course, that we immediately become *fully* enlightened; but at least we have made a true beginning when we can gaze around at all the possessions, qualities, and capacities that are supposed to be ours and recognize that they do not really belong to us. In fact, a good exercise for us beginners is to scan slowly over the world we have built around us and say of every item in it, "Not mine; just on temporary loan": "This house—not mine, just on temporary loan; those books—not mine, just on temporary loan; these fingers—not mine, just on temporary loan; my mind—not mine, just on temporary loan." It takes a long time to carry out this exercise properly, but when it is done properly the result is a clear mind and a light heart.

> **Once we realize that we own absolutely nothing, we are enlightened, not only in the sense that our minds are flooded with light, but also in the sense that a weight is lifted from us and our hearts grow lighter.**

Such a turning toward enlightenment is recorded again and again in the life stories of holy persons, particularly those of the Buddhist tradition. We are told, for example, of how 2,500 years ago a prince of the Sakya clan in Nepal, of the Gautama family, Siddhartha by personal name and known to history as the Buddha (i.e. "enlightened one"), came to exactly such a moment.

Until he was twenty-nine years old, he had been protected by his father from awareness of the transitory nature of human life; he was secure in his royal status, his riches, his health, his beautiful wife, and his son. Then one day he succeeded in evading his father's protective screen; he drove out of the eastern gate of the palace on a pleasure excursion in the company of his charioteer only to be confronted by the sight of an old man. Siddhartha realized that youth was not something he could own.

Another day he drove out of the southern gate and saw a desperately sick man; and Siddhartha realized that health was not something he could own. A third day, when he drove out of the western gate, he saw a corpse; then he realized that his very life was not his own. Finally he drove out of the northern gate where he saw a monk with a shaven head dressed in a tattered yellow robe. "What man is this?" he asked and was told that the man was a homeless wanderer, seeking for nothing but holiness.

That night Siddhartha lay awake while all others in the royal palace slept. Then he arose, bade farewell to his sleeping wife and his beautiful son, and went out with his charioteer into the darkness and silence. At the edge of the forest he cut off his long black hair and handed it to his charioteer to take back to the palace. Alone now, he took off his princely robes and put on the robes of a homeless beggar, a seeker after nothing but holiness.

This turning toward the light, which we observe here in the case of the Buddha, finds its parallels in many religious traditions. One obvious parallel is that of Saul on the road to Damascus, though it was even more dramatic in his case than in Siddhartha's. Saul was such an obstinate creature that it was necessary for God to seize him by the scruff of his neck and fling him to the ground and strike him blind before he would turn toward the light. And even then it took him many years before the light permeated the whole of his being and he could be described as truly enlightened.

That something similar to the experience of the Buddha and of Paul happens to all of us in search of wholeness was well recognized by medieval writers when they wrote the lives of saints. Anyone who has read many medieval lives of saints will have been struck by the fact that these accounts of holy people follow a regular pattern, according to which there are two supremely important moments in every person's life. The first is the moment of turning or conversion (which is, after all, only another word for turning) such as we have referred to in the case of the Buddha and of St. Paul; and the second is the act of dying. Clearly the two are so essentially connected in the minds of the writers as to be virtually one act: the manner of a person's death is the measure of how sincerely and utterly that person turned toward the light at the moment of conversion.

Once the turning has begun in us, we recognize that, even though we may not have realized it at the time, it was truly a dramatic and crucial moment in our lives, a true turning point. As one convert put it:

> After one moment when I bowed my head
> And the whole world turned over and came
>   upright....[16]

But the drama does not end at that moment; for, as we have seen, if one is converted, turned around, one is turned toward the reality of death. That reality was pointed to by Jesus, of whom it is written, "The moment came for his assumption to be accomplished and he set his face toward Jerusalem...."[17] Knowing that Jerusalem, for him, spelled death, Jesus set his face straight toward it.

In Jesus we have an example of a person who was utterly turned toward the light.

In Jesus we have an example of a person who was utterly turned toward the light. But for most of us that turning is much more gradual and requires that we do it by degrees, day in and day out. Because the sinner is heading in absolutely the wrong direction, he has to turn, through a 180-degree angle. And usually that does not happen quickly; when it does, as in the case of Saul, there are violent repercussions:

---

16. G. K. Chesterton, in his poem, *The Convert*.
17. Luke 9:51.

he is flung to the ground, he loses his sight, and for three days is unable to eat or drink.

For most people this turning is more gradual; and for them, as beginners, there is scarcely any exercise so helpful spiritually as the Muslim practice of turning physically toward the Holy Place. Five times each day a devout Muslim will turn his body toward Mecca and in so doing the whole of his being, mind and heart as well as body, is being set toward the Holy One. Hence, in every truly Muslim building, we see the *qiblah,* a small recess in the wall that indicates the direction of the Holy Place. By that seemingly small act of turning the body toward the *qiblah,* day in and day out, the devout Muslim gradually turns his whole being toward the Holy Place where the Holy One dwells.

A similar function is served for believers in the Orthodox Christian tradition by the positioning of icons. In each room in the house of a pious Russian, for instance, there is established an icon corner—a corner of the room where some icon is positioned, and toward which anyone entering the room turns almost automatically. Among believing Jews it is the practice to fix a *mesuzah* to the doorpost of their houses; while even the meanest Hindu room invariably has a picture pinned up depicting some holy being which turns the minds and hearts of those dwelling in the room toward the reality of the divine.

Since this practice of establishing external signs to turn our minds and hearts toward the light in which we face death and holiness is so universal, it would be very presumptuous of any beginner along this path to imagine that he or she can dispense with such a sign. Sometimes, admittedly, people mistake the sign for the reality and cling to their icons or their holy pictures superstitiously, but that does not invalidate the truth that we arrive at universal reality by performing particular acts.

There is a verse from the Koran which runs like a refrain throughout the centuries of Muslim piety: "Wherever you turn, there is the face of God."[18] But that verse has only acquired its full universal meaning for humankind through the millions upon millions of particular occasions when a humble Muslim has faithfully turned his body in prayer toward a particular *qiblah,* and hence toward the face of God.

In establishing such a sign within one's particular world it is less important to discover the perfect sign than to start off with one, no matter how imperfect. (So much time and energy is wasted in searching for what is perfect as an excuse for not doing what is good!) Then gradually you find the sign that is most in accordance with the aspirations of your own heart. Facing me as I write these lines, for instance, is a reproduction of a painting by Rembrandt, the painter who more than any other speaks to my condition. The picture is titled "The Return of the Prodigal Son," and was inspired, of course, by the parable of the prodigal son recorded by St. Luke in his Gospel.

In fact, the parable itself is often described as "the gospel within the Gospel," so perfectly does it represent the essence of Jesus' message. In the picture itself we see the prodigal son kneeling before his father, who is standing with his son's head resting against his breast; the father's

18. Koran, Sura II, 115.

loving hands are placed in blessing upon his son's shoulders, and as we look at the picture, we hear the son's words, "I will turn and go to my father and say to him, 'Father, I have sinned against God and against you....'" The picture, like the parable, is the perfect sign for anyone who has been touched to make a 180-degree turn, as the prodigal son did.

No commentary in words, of course, could exhaust the meaning that is enshrined in the picture, but some hint of what such an external sign can come to mean is given in a passage from the pen of Andrei Sinyavsky. This passage is all the more compelling when we know that it was written in the loneliness of a harsh Soviet labor camp by a man who had been converted from agnosticism to Christian belief. Sinyavsky wrote:

> Looking at Rembrandt's picture, we are confronted by the son's bare head, which is more expressive than many a human face—filthy, peeling like an onion, as scabby as a convict's pate, exuding repentance. Nothing in the picture is directed toward the spectator. Like the main characters in it, it is turned to the wall—into itself. Verily: everything is within you. As a result, no picture could be more relevant to the theme of the Church.
>
> All is submerged in that munificent cathedral darkness more deeply than Sadko [a character from a Russian folktale] sitting on the bottom of the sea. And it is a good thing that the paint has become so dark over the years. When it becomes so dark that we can no longer see it all, then the Prodigal Son will rise from his knees and, turning, reveal his face. [19]

---

19. Andrei Sinyavsky, pen name Abraham Tertz, *A Voice from the Chorus* (London, 1976), p. 99.

When the prodigal son does, indeed, turn round and reveal his face, we shall find, written among the lines of that face, the second truth that beginners need to know at the outset of this undertaking, which is the cost of holiness.

For holiness is, quite succinctly, as the poet says,

A condition of complete simplicity
(Costing not less than everything).[20]

Moreover, by "everything" the poet literally means everything. And he is right. Sooner or later everything has to go; what is then left is a holy person. It is like a person who comes across a treasure in a field who then goes and sells everything in order to buy the field for the sake of the treasure. Or like the merchant in search of precious pearls who comes across the most precious of all and sells everything for the sake of that pearl.

For the sake of holiness there is nothing that may not be demanded of a seeker. Take the case of Daito Kokushi. Because of a crippled leg, he had been unable for many years to sit in the full lotus position for meditation, a position that, within his tradition, was considered virtually indispensable for enlightenment. On January 21, 1338, feeling his death approaching, he seated himself on his meditation seat, broke his crippled leg by his own strength, and so was able to assume the full lotus posture. Then he seized his calligraphy brush and composed some lines—for he was a poet by vocation; at his last stroke the brush fell from his hand, and he died.

Or take the more subtly demanding case of Zen master Hakuin. Here it was not physical well being that was at

---

20. T. S. Eliot, *Little Gidding.*

stake, but something that touches one even more intimately, that is, one's good name. Master Hakuin was a famous and revered Zen teacher who lived as a hermit. One day a well-to-do young woman in a neighboring fishing village, on discovering herself to be pregnant, announced that, for all his great pretensions to holiness, it was none other than Zen Master Hakuin who was responsible for her condition. At this news all the people of the village, led by the girl's relatives, marched angrily up the mountain to Hakuin's hut and, amid shouts and mockery, accused Hakuin of being the father of the child. "Is that so?" was all Hakuin said. Then, when the woman's delivery time came round, he took the child into his hut and nurtured it, washed it, and cared for it as his very own.

Some eighteen months later, the child's mother was overcome by her guilty conscience and confessed that, in fact, the father of the child was not Hakuin but a local young fisherman. At this all the village people were overcome with shame, and once more, led by the girl's relatives, they processed up the mountain to Hakuin's hut, making great protestations of sorrow for having taken away the holy man's reputation. They assured Hakuin that they now realized he was not the father of the child. "Is that so?" was all Hakuin said.[21]

A similar incident occurred in the life of the fourteenth-century Dominican holy man, Heinrich Suso. Although still young, Heinrich, the wandering preacher, had acquired a reputation for sanctity until a scheming woman left her newly

---

21. C. Naranjo and R. E. Ornstein, *On the Psychology of Meditation* (New York, 1971), p. 24.

born babe on the doorstep of his lodgings and spread the rumor that he was the father. Just as Hakuin did, so Heinrich took the child and cradled it, saying, "My beautiful, dear, tender child, I will take care of you, for you are God's child and mine too. So long as God gives me a single mouthful, I will share it with you to the glory of God; and I will bear patiently whatever may happen to me on your account." What Heinrich had to bear was calumny from all sides, even from many religious who proved only too ready to point scornful fingers at him, and mock his reputation for holiness. Not until the accusing woman lay at death's door did she confess and Heinrich's good name was restored to him.[22]

Perhaps the realization that one's spiritual call may well destroy one's good name is particularly vital for those of us who are beginners, because we are especially vulnerable to the temptation of holiness. By this I mean that it is very easy for us to believe that all we have to do is to carry on with our usual comfortable, self-satisfied lives; only now that we have become interested in spiritual things we just cast a halo around our comfortable selves and our usual lives as a kind of spiritual *decor.*

A devastating exposé of such self-deception is to be found in the climax of Georges Bernanos' novel *Star of Satan.* The central character of the novel, Father Donissan, is the saintly parish priest of the village of Lumbres who, in spite of the suspicion of the ecclesiastical authorities, has acquired a reputation as a worker of miraculous reconciliations through his endless hours of listening to penitents in the confessional.

---

22. S. M. C., *Henry Suso: Saint and Poet* (Oxford, 1947), pp. 69–76.

Toward the end of the novel, there comes upon the scene a famous French writer, a member of the Académie Française who is celebrated for his skillful irony. Already author of the "The Paschal Candle," in which he showed himself to be toying with the idea of "conversion," Antoine Saint-Martin, as he is called, makes a pilgrimage to the village of Lumbres. There he goes into the village church musing on how he may now take from the curé a taste of the sanctity fitting for such a famous writer as himself in the evening of his days—a good way of rounding off his remarkable life. "How pleasant," he reflects, "so late in life, to experience the joys of initiation!" And he pictures to himself the literary public piously admiring the scene: the philosopher and the saint of Lumbres side by side in their rural solitude.

Strolling alone in the evening light down the aisle of the church, cultivating his sense of peace, the author of "The Paschal Candle" inquisitively pulls open the door of the confessional. There, the first thing that meets his eyes is a pair of rough shoes and the fold of a soutane caught up into an odd shape, a long, thin leg in a woolen stocking, stretched out stiff, a heel resting on the threshold. Dead at his post, the curé of Lumbres:

> ...this silly unexpected old man angered Antoine Saint-Martin quite as much as he scared him. Since after all, here he was being disturbed at an auspicious moment, in the midst of his fantasy: the last word now remained with that singular witness, ensconced in his dark box, this standing corpse. A professor of irony had found his master, and been awakened, shamefaced, from rather a

foolish dream, a pathetic dream.... And though the dark
mouth in the shadow, which had the look of a gaping
wound torn open by the burst of a last cry, gave forth no
sound, the body itself from head to foot was set in a posture of terrible defiance. "You sought my peace!" cried
the saint. "Come and get it."[23]

These are only a few illustrations of what holiness
costs. It always costs not less than everything; but what
that "everything" is we do not dis-
cover until the moment when we
realize that we must let it go. "It
means everything to me," we often
say when we are speaking about
our health, or our good name, or
some loving relationship. But we
have seen that Daito Kokushi had
to let his leg go, Hakuin and Suso
had to let their good names go, and
the curé of Lumbres had to let go of
his very life.

> **Holiness always costs not less than everything; but what that "everything" is we do not discover until the moment when we realize that we must let it go.**

Yet this is the sort of cost that
cannot be calculated. How do you
calculate the cost of everything?
There is no way of measuring or
calculating it. It follows that there
is nothing more contrary to holi-
ness than the habit of calculation. It is quite crucial to
recognize this because the habit of calculation can easily

23. Georges Bernanos, *Star of Satan* (London, 1940), pp. 331–6.

disguise itself as virtue. Indeed we at first find it shocking, when in reading *The Brothers Karamazov* we discover that Ivan's habit of keeping a reckoning of what he owes to his patrons is not a virtue in Dostoyevsky's eyes, whereas his brother Alyosha's habit of carelessly failing to reckon is. Or, as Dostoyevsky puts it:

> This strange trait in Alyosha's character must not, I think, be criticized too severely, for at the slightest acquaintance with him anyone would have perceived that Alyosha was one of those youths, almost of the type of religious enthusiast, who, if they were suddenly to come into possession of a large fortune, would not hesitate to give it away for the asking, either for good works or perhaps to a clever rogue.... In later years Pyotr Alexandrovich Miusov, a man very sensitive on the score of money and bourgeois honesty, pronounced the following judgment, after getting to know Alyosha: "Here is perhaps the one man in the world whom you might leave alone without a penny, in the center of an unknown town of a million inhabitants, and he would not come to harm, he would not die of cold and hunger, for he would be fed and sheltered at once; and if he were not, he would find a shelter for himself, and it would cost him no effort or humiliation. And to shelter him would be no burden, but, on the contrary, would probably be looked on as a pleasure."[24]

As a gloss upon that passage in the novel, one may say that Ivan grew more and more egotistic because of his habit of calculation. For when a human being starts to calculate, the factor in the calculation to which one invariably

---

24. *The Brothers Karamazov*, bk. 1, ch. 4.

attaches the highest value is one's own ego. But, when a
person realizes that the cost of holiness is beyond calculation, then one's ego does not come into reckoning; on the
contrary it drifts away into irrelevance. At this point, however, when we recognize that the cost of our undertaking is
beyond calculation, we may run into the danger of fearing
that too much is being demanded of us. In which case, we
are likely to fall prey to discouragement.

Yet, it is precisely when we have been brought to this
point of danger that we learn to appreciate most deeply a
fundamental truth which cannot fail to be an endless
source of encouragement: that is, before ever any of God's
creatures longs for holiness, God himself longs for every
single one of his creatures to be holy. The ground of love, as
St. John says, lies not in our love for God but in his having
loved us from the beginning.[25]

Of all the truths that we have to try to realize in our
undertaking, none is more vital than this; yet much religious teaching in the past has virtually denied it. In such
perverted teaching, God is represented as a sort of cor-
rectional officer who has no desire to see his charges
reform and be liberated, but is actually pleased when he
can mark up some misdeed against them and confirm to
himself their sinfulness. How utterly different is St.
Paul's teaching when he writes, "Blessed be God our gentle Father, Father of our Lord Jesus Christ and the God
of all consolations who consoles us in all our sorrows so
that we may be able to console those who are in sorrow

---

25. 1 John 4:10.

by the same consolation with which we are comforted by God...."[26]

For St. Paul, God is not a severe taskmaster but a "gentle Father." Moreover, it is worth noticing that the Hebrew word underlying the phrase translated as "of all consolations" is probably *rahamin*, the root meaning of which is "womb." God loves mankind not only with a father's love, but also with the longing of a mother for the child of her womb.

Since the truth St. Paul is here expressing is fundamental, the ways of expressing it are inexhaustible. For instance, a contemporary scientist, approaching it from a different perspective, has written: "We are not independent entities, alien to earth. The earth in turn is not adrift in a vacuum unrelated to the cosmos. The cosmos itself is no longer cold and hostile—because it is *our* universe. It brought us forth and it maintains our being. We are, in the very literal sense of the words, children of the universe."[27] In other words, at the very center of the universe is a loving Heart whose longings are the source of our own hearts' longings. Hence, our own longings can never be in vain, because they correspond with reality, with that Heart upon which our universe is centered.

As has already been said, we can never be discouraged so long as we realize this truth, because it means quite

---

26. 2 Corinthians 1:3–7.

27. Eric J. Chaisson, "The Scenario of Cosmic Evolution" in *Harvard Magazine,* Nov./Dec. 1977, pp. 21–33. Cf. also the remarks of the Princeton physicist Freeman Dyson in a BBC broadcast on Dec. 12, 1979: "I do not feel like an alien in this universe. The more I study the details of its architecture the more evidence I find that the universe in some sense must have known we were coming."

literally that not even the slightest honest effort upon our part is ever wasted, but eventually bears fruit. How vital this realization is becomes clear when we reflect upon how many frustrations we experience every day of our lives, as a result of which it can sometimes seem as though our lives are nothing but an endless series of frustrations. Only by faith that at the center of the universe is a loving Heart can we know that these frustrations are not in vain. Though occasionally a veil is lifted, and we are granted a glimpse of how such frustrations do in fact bear fruit.

Only by faith that at the center of the universe is a loving Heart can we know that frustrations are not in vain.

Many people have been granted such a glimpse through the example of Jean Vianney, the Curé d'Ars. For although this country priest eventually became one of the most famous and influential saints of the nineteenth century, nevertheless, because he was so slow at his studies, it was at one time touch-and-go whether he would even be admitted to ordination. He was especially slow in Latin, a language that was essential, of course, for priests in those days. No sooner had the young man got a Latin word into his head than he forgot it again.

But for years he kept on plowing through the daily frustration of trying to acquire this intractable language. He never really managed it; and he was only allowed to be ordained in the end through the complaisance of an easy-going bishop. Yet, within a few years this same Curé d'Ars was famous as the wisest confessor in Europe. Aching for his reconciling words, thousands of penitents lined up each day outside his confessional box, so that he often had to spend eighteen hours a day sitting there and listening to them. The one who had never been able to master words could now transmit the only word that matters, the word of healing.

One would have to be blind not to see the connection between all those days, weeks, months, and years of frustration when the young seminarian was vainly trying to learn Latin and all those miraculously fruitful years when the Curé d'Ars was bringing peace and healing to thousands of brokenhearted sinners. The frustrations were not impediments to the work of healing but conditions for it, the soil that the young seminarian had to till before the fruit could be borne.

All the same, Jean Vianney could never have carried on through those years of frustration if he had simply been acting out of a sense of duty or as a way of perfecting his own soul. Only a deep longing to be one with God by serving him could possibly have carried him through—a longing, moreover, of such a sort as we seem to encounter rarely in the Anglo-Saxon world. In fact, it was not until I found myself in the world of Islam that I ever realized how one might long for God in a way analogous to the way that a human lover longs for the beloved when separated from him. The notion of serving God with which I was familiar was of doing his will or fulfilling one's duty, and thereby loving him. But the realization that the call to holiness is the echo of God's longing for each one of us, or that our search begins, continues, and ends in longing, only came to me when I heard the voice of Islam.

It was in the deep darkness of a bitingly frosty January morning in the Holy Land, near Nazareth. As I lay shivering with cold, waiting for the break of dawn, in a hostel high above the town, I suddenly heard the cry of the muezzin from the mosque hundreds of feet below: "*Allahu akhbar*—God is great—prayer is better than sleep." Those words I had heard many times before, but this time they arose out of another world and were addressed to another world. The cry came out of a heart that would never rest content with earthly satisfactions. It pierced the thick darkness and stillness of the early hours, echoing and re-echoing around the hills in which Nazareth is cupped. The cry was sustained for some quarter of an hour; and even when it ceased and silence fell upon Nazareth once more, the message continued to reverberate within me: only One can satisfy longing of such depth and intensity. No creature can do so, but only the Creator.

The call that I heard in Nazareth is not a call of the same type that we humans experience through the urge for food, say, or for drink or sex. Such urges can be satisfied, in an earthly way, by food and drink and sex. But the longing for holiness is a call to absolute union with the Holy One and comes from beyond this earth. So it can only be satisfied from beyond. For the same reason it is a call to a unique, exclusive relationship.

As a token of this unique relationship we are told, in the Book of Revelation, that the Holy One gives each of us a white stone, "and in the stone a new name written

which no one knows except the one who receives it."[28]
The name referred to is the unique call that every creature
receives, for which no other crea-
ture, however saintly, can respond.
For instance, however saintly she
was, Mother Teresa could not have
served as a substitute for either the
author of this book or for you who
are reading it. Evidently God did
not want two Mother Teresas, but
longs for the author of this book
and the reader each to become as
uniquely holy as she became. Nor
can any creature enter directly
into the relationship of another
creature with the Holy One; so in
that sense the relationship is an
exclusive one.

> **Evidently God did
> not want two
> Mother Teresas,
> but longs for the
> author of this book
> and the reader each
> to become as
> uniquely holy as
> she became.**

But, by one of those paradoxes
in which the spiritual world abounds, it is in virtue of one's
exclusive relationship to the Holy One that one can
include, or embrace, all other creatures. To embrace means
to put one's arms around, to envelop in some way, and to
do this one has to go beyond, to transcend the creature one
wishes to embrace. If one did not get beyond one would be
stuck, as if one's feet were in glue, incapable of reaching
around any other creature. Only by responding to one's
unique, exclusive call from the Holy One can one move

---

28. Revelation 2:17.

toward an inclusive, all-embracing relationship with all other creatures.

As beginners, therefore, in the world of holy beings, we have the great encouragement of knowing that our call into this world comes from the Holy One himself who longs for each of us to become holy even as he is holy. We have also learned that it is a simple matter, indeed a matter of simplicity, "costing not less than everything." What it will eventually cost us to let go of everything that we regard as our own is beyond calculation. Also beyond calculation is what we shall become through letting go—"we are children of God even now," as St. John says, "but what we shall eventually be has not yet been shown. But we know that when he comes we shall be like him for we shall see him as he is. For everyone who hopes in this way becomes holy, even as he is holy."[29]

Finally, all of these truths are beautifully contained in a story from ancient India:

> Mount Kailasha is the abode of Lord Shiva and his wife, Parvati. Once Shiva and Parvati were sitting on the top of Mount Kailasha enjoying the cool air and looking at the vast plains where there were cities, towns, jungles, rivers. Parvati said, "My Lord, look! Thousands of your devotees are singing in temples, living in jungles, caves, or by the riverbanks meditating on you. Why don't you give salvation to those who are so devotional and loving?" Shiva said, "My dear, let us go and see those devotees. Now I am ready to give them salvation."

---

29. 1 John 2:2–3.

Shiva disguised himself as a saint and Parvati as his disciple. They came down to the world and entered a town. They sat in a secluded place, and if anyone came to the saint he would tell the person his past and future. In no time the word spread all over the adjoining towns that a high saint with powers of prophecy had arrived. Flocks of people eager to know their futures began to collect. One day a group of devotees came. They were singing and dancing, and all were intoxicated with devotion. After chanting, one devotee, who appeared to be the leader of the group, came forward, and bowed to the saint. Very meekly he said, "Guru Maharaj, will you tell me when I will get salvation? I meditate in the winter for two and one half hours, sitting in water up to my neck. During summer, I meditate for two and one half hours surrounded by fires. When it rains, I sit in the rain and meditate. I meditate every day for eight hours, and for several years I have been taking only a single meal of fruits and milk each day."

The saint looked at him with much surprise and said, "Oh, you are doing hard austerities! You are a very good yogi. You have much devotion." Hearing this the man felt very good and was excited to hear about his salvation. The saint continued, "If you go on doing your *sadhana* regularly, you can get salvation after three births." The devotee was shocked at hearing this. With bowed head he went back to his group saying, "Still three births!"

Another man spoke about his *sadhana,* and the saint told him it would be seven births. In this way everyone asked about getting salvation. The saint told one ten births, another fifteen, others twenty or thirty.

Finally, when all were finished, a small, thin, ugly man who had been hiding behind the others came forward. He was shy and afraid but he dared to say, "Sir, I don't do any *sadhana,* but I love his creation, and I try not to hurt anyone by my actions, thoughts, or words. Can I get salvation?"

The saint looked at the little man and then scratched his head as if he were in some doubt. The man again bowed to the saint and nervously said, "Can I, sir?" The saint then said, "Well, if you go on loving God in the same way, maybe after a thousand births you too will get salvation."

As soon as the man heard that he could eventually get salvation, he screamed with joy, "I can get salvation! I can get salvation!" And he began to dance in ecstasy. All of a sudden his body changed into a flame. At the same time, the saint and his disciple also changed into flames. All three flames merged into one and disappeared.

Shiva and Parvati were again sitting on the top of Mount Kailasha. Parvati said, "My Lord, I am very confused. You told the leader, who does such hard austerities, that he would get salvation in three births. Then you told the ugly man that he would get salvation in a thousand births, but you gave it to him instantly." Shiva said, "No doubt the first devotee had much devotion and was doing austerities sincerely, but he still had an ego about his *sadhana.* He had not surrendered his ego yet, and three births appeared a very long time to him. The other man had so much faith that even a thousand births were very short for him. He completely surrendered to me. I did not give him salvation; it was his own faith in my words. His emotions increased so much that he could not keep the body any longer. His essence of life, the Self, took abode in me."[30]

From this story it can be seen that sometimes beginners are near to their end. And another thing is for sure: anyone who regards himself as already holy still has a long way to go.

---

30. Baba Hari Dass, *Silence Speaks* (Santa Cruz, 1977), pp. 23–5.

5

Responsibility

—

WE HAVE ALREADY SEEN, IN THE CHAPTER ON "OUR PLACE IN Creation," how Pascal was frightened by the silence of the infinite spaces. Many other people, both previously and since, have been overwhelmed by the contemplation of those infinite spaces with a sense of their own total insignificance. When there are all those thousands of miles of earth around us, and the earth is merely one tiny planet in a universe where there are infinite suns and planets, and since this universe began 20,000 million years ago, what possible significance can be attached to the five or six feet of matter that is me and which lasts only a pitiable seventy years? I am no more than a speck of dust or, at best, a firefly.

That is one way of looking at it; but it is the wrong way. It fails to see that responsibility is also a reality and that it is not cancelled out by the immensity of space and time. Once you accept responsibility as a reality, you realize that the immensity of space and time, far from canceling out one's own responsibility, actually intensifies it. Responsibility is rather like one of those burning glasses that you point toward the sun; it picks up the sun's rays and concentrates them into a point of intense heat—as you can feel if you direct it toward your skin, or as you see if you use it to set paper afire. The vaster the distance out in space the more intense the heat on your skin as the light passes through the glass of responsibility.

Admittedly, each of us on this earth's surface, when caught in the lens of an air-photographer from a height of 10,000 feet, seems to be no more than a speck of dust. But from where we stand we know differently. Aware of the endless matter around us, stretching beyond our imagination, we know nevertheless that in the midst of it all there is one fragment—a piece of flesh, often rather battered, our body—which we now occupy and for which we are totally responsible. We cannot control the matter of a million years ago, or the matter of a hundred years from now. But for this matter that I occupy here and now, the frail and vulnerable matter that is my body, I am totally responsible.

For this matter that I occupy here and now, the frail and vulnerable matter that is my body, I am totally responsible.

Recognizing that it is this piece of matter, and no other, for which I am directly and totally responsible leads me also to realize that it is unique and therefore infinitely precious for the time that it lasts. It is a gift from the

Creator in co-operation with all those beings who throughout millions of years have struggled and suffered in handing on to me this form of matter which is a human body, with eyes to see, and lips to speak, and ears to hear—with all the faculties, in fact, that have been shaped to create a human being.

This matter of which I speak is the matter of holiness. For what we do with our bodies, what we put into them, how we treat them, what use we make of them, these are spiritual tasks that we are called to carry out in the name of holiness. There is no division in reality between the material and the spiritual; our spirituality is manifested by our treatment of matter. It is no accident, for instance, that all the great religions have promulgated regulations concerning the proper use of food; what you eat is not a trivial or indifferent matter; to put into your body some substance which you know to be harmful to your body is an act of ingratitude toward all those beings who have been in groaning and travail to give you birth, ingratitude toward the Creator particularly.

One could go around each part of the body showing how no act we perform with any of them is trivial, but that each one is charged with spiritual significance. Think of the tongue, for instance. We are responsible for every single word that we utter with our tongues; and if we utter bitter words we not only harm others, we also harm our own bodies. Our bitterness produces chemical changes in our bodies that harm them; and if such bitter speech is continually repeated, the body will eventually declare itself diseased as a form of protest. No wonder the great prophet

Isaiah, before he opened his mouth to prophesy, had to have his tongue touched with a burning coal, brought by a seraph from the holy altar, before his tongue was pure enough to speak the Word of God.

Within the limits of our circumstances, we are totally responsible for the use of our tongues, our sexual members, our ears and every other bodily member.

In the same way, all the great religions place tremendous emphasis on the proper use of our sexual members. And rightly so, for even leaving aside the effect on the other partner involved through using our sexual member, it is clear that whatever we do with this intensely sensitive organ produces deep reverberations within our own bodies. (This truth is strangely ignored in many countries where electors choose politicians to govern them who cannot even govern their own sexual members.)

A further instance of the need to take responsibility for what we allow to enter our bodies concerns our hearing faculties. Since the human body is a composition of infinitely delicate and finely balanced vibrations, one of our obligations is to maintain that fine balance, which in its turn requires us to screen it, so far as we can, from destructive vibrations. It is well known for instance that sounds of a certain high frequency can so shake the delicate balance of the body as actually to shatter its composition entirely. So it is not a matter of indifference, for instance, what kind of music we choose to hear. Even at the physical level, and correspondingly at the spiritual level, there are some sounds in music that are destructive and there are some that are edifying. We have to learn to become attuned to which is which, and to choose to allow only the edifying into our bodies. Within the limits of our circumstances, therefore, we are totally responsible for the use of our tongues, our sexual members, our ears and every other bodily member.

Not so often recognized is humanity's responsibility in the matter of the inanimate creation and of living creatures, a responsibility that arises from our position in the universe as the beneficiaries of earth's riches and inheritors of the capacities developed over millions of years by myriads of living creatures. Man has been designated by God as the head of creation, the creature in whom the struggles of all previous creatures are recapitulated. "Open your mouth for the dumb," says God in the Book of Proverbs, "for the rights of all who are left unprotected."[31]

Typical of how we ignore this divine charge was an incident that I observed some time ago. I was present at Mass in a village hall one hot summer's day. While the Mass was proceeding, a wasp was buzzing up and down inside one of the windows of the hall, trying to get out. It was doing no harm to anyone, but it was annoying the stout, middle-aged lady in front of me, one of the pillars of the church. Eventually she seized the *Universe,* a Catholic newspaper, rolled it up tightly and strode across to the window. Then,

31. Proverbs 31:8.

just as the priest was uttering the words, "Blessed are You, Lord, God of all creation," she struck the wasp dead.

At the very moment when the whole congregation was blessing God for all creation, the woman had arbitrarily destroyed one of God's creatures. I cannot imagine what St. Isaac the Syrian would have made of her; he says that whoever has a charitable heart "cannot see or call to mind a creature without his eyes being filled with tears by reason of the immense compassion which seizes his heart."[32]

It was a spiritual kinsman of St. Isaac, Father Zossima of *The Brothers Karamazov,* who showed how our direct responsibility for our own bodies and for dumb creatures might indirectly stretch yet further. In his final conversations, Father Zossima describes how our very faces may indirectly produce momentous consequences. He asks us to think of a child walking down a street, rather bewildered by the evil in the world and searching for signs that life has meaning. If we have over the years allowed our hearts to become embittered, that will be reflected in our faces. So when the child has seen our face, the image that will remain in his heart will be of evil and meaninglessness. It may turn out that our face has sown a seed of evil in the child that will one day overgrow his whole heart. On the other hand, if we have over the years filled our hearts with love, that also will be reflected in our faces and the passing child in the street will be encouraged by what he sees to find meaning in life.[33]

32. Quoted in A. M. Allchin, *The Kingdom of Love and Knowledge* (London, 1979), p. 202.

33. *The Brothers Karamazov,* bk. 6, ch. 3.

Such an illustration is by no means imaginary. We have from the pen of Olivier Clément a moving account of how a face saved his life. It was in the days when he was an atheist, though an unhappy one. He was so unhappy, in fact, and so oppressed by the meaninglessness of human life that he was seriously thinking of committing suicide. Then one day as he was walking depressed beside the Mediterranean seashore his attention was riveted by the face of someone who was passing by. The person's face was radiant with meaning, full of such goodness as can only come from years of cultivating a loving heart. In a twinkling Clément's suicidal thoughts were dispelled and a seed sown in his heart that was eventually to transform him into an ardent believer.[34] Not surprisingly, Clément asserts with warm conviction that there is a branch of theology that is properly described as "a theology of faces."

It is obviously somewhat daunting to acknowledge that our responsibility for our own body can indirectly have such consequences, but it is still more daunting to realize that even the corpse we leave behind at death may influence the people who gaze upon it; and in that sense we are responsible for our bodies even after death. As proof of this, consider the case of the French writer George Bernanos. All his life Bernanos had been wracked by a great fear of death, with which he had wrestled most courageously. When he finally died in 1948, after an agonizing illness, his corpse was laid out so that people could pay

34. Olivier Clément, *Dialogues avec le Patriarche Athénagore* (Paris, 1969), p. 181.

their last respects. Pierre Bourdau was one of these, and of
that occasion he wrote:

> The cause that Bernanos served was as wide as the uni-
> verse. Such men will not have lived in vain, since their
> image is before our eyes to renew our confidence, when
> we are afraid to see humanity reduced to the law of num-
> bers, of statistics, and of material gain. If I ever need a
> fresh assurance that the destiny and glory of mankind is
> not to be contained within these dismal limits, it will be
> enough to recall the luminous vision of a face where the
> last act of a serene faith was to wipe out sixty years of
> suffering and bequeath to mankind, in exchange for this
> long ordeal, a smile of victory and ineffable promise.[35]

It would indeed seem, then, that we are even responsible for the corpse that we leave behind. Conversely, one
might ask, are we in some way responsible at the other end
of our lives, for the body that we take over at our conception? The answer, according to the Hindu and Buddhist
traditions, is yes. These traditions maintain that there is a
connection between one's condition in this present life and
one's actions in a previous life: in accordance with the law
of karma, the law of cause and effect, those previous
actions leave *skandhas,* or traces, which are the elements
that compose one's body in this present life.

Now whatever one's judgment of the metaphysical psychology at the back of the Hindu-Buddhist tradition, one
cannot deny that it induces a tremendous sense of responsibility for one's own condition. There can be no excuses

---

35. R. Speaight, *Georges Bernanos* (London, 1973), p. 274.

for one's condition, no escape, no blaming of anyone else. And in those who thoroughly understand the tradition it provokes a fierce determination to act in such a way that the *skandhas* are eliminated in this life. Then one is no longer caught on the wheel of rebirth; one is liberated, enlightened, in nirvana.

Recently a Zen Buddhist has written an account of the fierce determination with which she assumed responsibility for all her acts both in her present and in her previous lives. She is Jiyu Kennet, the English-born abbess of the Zen Buddhist monastery of Mount Shasta in Northern California, and her book is entitled *How to Grow a Lotus*.[36] In it, she tells us that when a doctor informed her she probably had no more than a few months to live, she immediately determined to "clean up" her life. By this she meant that she was going to sit and meditate and totally recall every instance in the past when she had failed to fulfill the precepts of the Buddha.

So she resigned her office as abbess of Shasta and moved down to the little Buddhist temple in Oakland. In almost complete isolation, she sat meditating day and night, envisaging her past life, writing down her observations, and drawing the images that accompanied them. Gradually, the fierce ray of truth which she directed upon her past acts seems to have burnt up many of the traces left upon her by those acts, and she became enlightened—her body itself became lighter and threw off the illness which threatened to kill her. Not that it mattered to her, by this

---

36. Jiyu Kennet, *How to Grow a Lotus* (Mt. Shasta, 1977).

time, whether she lived or died. All that mattered was to
know the truth about herself: once you attain the truth it
doesn't matter when your body dies since your life is
already consummated.

Even for those who do not belong to the Buddhist tradition, this story of Jiyu Kennet provides a model of how
one should assume total responsibility for one's condition
and how one should "clean up" one's life. In light of it, for
instance, I myself focused attention upon certain actions I
had taken thirty years ago, in my twenties. Those actions I
now see as contravening the precepts of my religious tradition. At the time I did not see the truth of the matter so
clearly; and so it would be very easy for me to excuse them
as the vagaries of a young man. Even though allowances
may be made for a young man's vagaries, nevertheless,
objectively, my actions left *skandhas,* or traces upon me, in
accordance with the law of *karma.* Unless I recognize that
those *skandhas* are still elements in my composition, and
unless I assume responsibility for burning them out, in
some way they will continue to be repeated in one life after
another (perhaps those of my children's children?).

Another illustration of the same point, which many
people have vaguely sensed, arises out of the life-stories of
war heroes. These, in their younger days, performed heroically in wartime, bombing, shooting, and sinking hordes of
their country's enemies. For this they were greatly praised.
Even though subjectively they felt that what they were
doing was right, yet objectively the truth is that killing
other beings produces *karma.* However well intentioned
the brave men may have been, for them there is no escape

from the consequences of killing. Hence many of these war heroes find themselves in confusion during their later years; the very deeds for which they are publicly acclaimed are the source of confusion and agony within themselves, and this is made all the worse because the acclaim almost inevitably blinds them and prevents them from recognizing the true source of their disturbance.

In fact, one of the reasons for beginning the practice of holiness with a consideration of responsibility is that confusion over the matter can easily prevent us from assuming full responsibility for our lives, a failure that immediately hamstrings us in our practice. And one of the features of responsibility that sometimes proves difficult to grasp is that it includes not only a subjective, personal aspect, but also an objective, representative aspect.

I was first led to see this as a result of the years I spent as a marriage counselor. During that time I gradually came to see that there was one factor in marital troubles that the textbooks on the subject hardly noticed and certainly did not analyze sufficiently. That is to say, in almost all cases of marital breakdown, I had an uneasy feeling that one or other of the partners seemed to put up with more from the other partner than he or she should have. But it was difficult for me to find any ground for this feeling, since the "suffering" partner so very often appeared to be noble and to be putting up with the partner's bad behavior quite heroically.

Then one day, after listening to a sorrowful tale from one of the "sufferers," I myself could not put up with it any longer and I exploded—silently exclaiming, "No human being should allow himself to be treated like that! As far as you personally are concerned you can put up with it, if you like. That's your business! But you should never allow humanity to be insulted in that way. That's our business as well!" In the sufferer's person the image of man was being insulted and that somehow involved the whole of mankind. In other words, I saw that in all our actions there is both a personal and a representative element. Or, as the rabbis so neatly express it: "If I am here, then the whole of mankind is here." Which is not, as may seem at first, an arrogant statement, but a sober formulation of a basic truth.

Since what the rabbis say is true, then every action of human beings, whether they like it or not, is normative, is speaking for the whole of mankind. In this sense, each one of us, whether we like it or not, is a teacher in all our actions, each one of which is implicitly proposing itself as a norm for the whole of mankind. So the responsibility for teaching is not confined to a particular group; it belongs to everybody. But a special responsibility rests upon those who publicly confess themselves to be representatives of those religious traditions that make holiness the goal of their adherents. On one occasion, Francis of Assisi himself was called to account on this when he

> **Each one of us, whether we like it or not, is a teacher in all our actions, each one of which is implicitly proposing itself as a norm for the whole of mankind.**

[p]assed through the field of a peasant who happened to be working there just then. The peasant ran over to him and asked solicitously if he were Brother Francis. When the man of God humbly replied that he was the man he was asking about, the peasant said: "Try to be as good as you are said to be by all men, for many put their trust in you, therefore I admonish you, never to be other than you are expected to be."[37]

In effect, what the peasant was saying to St. Francis is that each of us, in everything we do, is implicitly acting as representative of humanity. But further, since we are responding to a call that arises out of God's longing for our holiness, we are also the representatives of God, with all the responsibility that entails. We are made, so the Scriptures tell us, "in the image of God"; we are the *icon* of the invisible God, the glory of God. Incidentally, it is worth noticing that the word for "image" in the Hebrew of Genesis, *tselem,* has the root meaning of "shadow," whereas the connotation of the Greek word *icon,* used for "image" in the New Testament, is one of light and glory and radiance. In the process of enlightenment, from Genesis to Christ, humanity moves from the shadow into being an *icon* of God, radiating light.

Such an image of humanity radiating God is, of course, very attractive—seductively so in many instances, for human beings readily succumb to romantic images of themselves. We are only too prone to mistake the appearance for reality. But holiness is a matter of reality and not of appear-

---

37. Life of St. Francis, *2 Celano 142.*

ances, of being and not of pretending. Holiness means assuming total responsibility for all that we are and not simply for how we appear to other human beings—or even how we project ourselves to God. The classic formulation of this truth, of the inner reality, of the ineradicability of holiness, was given by St. John of the Cross when he wrote:

> He that with pure love works for God not only cares not whether or not men know it, but he does not even do these things so that God himself may know it. Such a person, even though it should never be known, would not cease to perform these same services and with the same gladness and love.[38]

It was through reflecting upon this truth formulated by St. John of the Cross that I myself once formulated what I consider to be a spiritual law: What you are always comes out; what you project rarely comes off. In illustration of this law, I would recount the following two stories: the first brings out the daunting side of the spiritual law, and the second shows the law to be an endless source of encouragement.

The first is set in Edinburgh during the 1950s. I was visiting my friend, Dr. Guth Badenoch, one afternoon at his home in George Square, and I mentioned to him how sad I was over the death of a child in the operating room of the nearby hospital. I then went on to say that I felt great sympathy for the doctor who had been in charge of the operation since he had encountered an unexpected complication and could hardly be blamed for what had eventually happened.

---

38. A. Peers (ed.), *Complete Works of St. John of the Cross,* vol. III (London, 1943), p. 257.

To my astonishment Dr. Badenoch, a just and understanding man, replied, "Oh, I don't know about that, Donald. I think the man is to blame. If anybody had handed me ether instead of chloroform I would have known from the weight that it was the wrong thing. You see, I know the man well. We were students together at Aberdeen, and he could have become one of the finest surgeons in Europe if only he had put his mind to it. But he didn't. He was more interested in golf. So he just used to do enough work to pass his examinations and no more. And that's how he has lived his life—just enough to get through, but no more. So he has never picked up those seemingly peripheral bits of knowledge that can one day be crucial. The other day in that operating room a bit of 'peripheral' knowledge was crucial and he didn't have it. But it wasn't the other day that he failed—it was thirty years ago, when he only gave himself half-heartedly to medicine."

It goes without saying that I found Dr. Badenoch's words a hard comment, and I do not know whether in this particular case they were justified. But fundamentally he was right: for almost a lifetime we may project an image of ourselves that enables us to get through, that deceives others and may even deceive us. In the end, however, what we are always comes out; and it is for what we are that we are responsible.

My second story is a happier one and concerns a priest, now dead, Fr. Gerald Culkin, a person who combined the finest features of both his Irish and his Yorkshire ancestry: steady, reliable, with a dry humor, but also passionate, imaginative, and of antique courtesy. When he was training for the priesthood in the early 1930s he had to study very hard so as to win grants that would allow him to make ends meet.

One day he happened to read a play by the Russian writer Chekhov, and was so entranced by it that he determined to learn Russian. He had no teacher, of course, and there were so few books and aids for lone learners in those days that setting out to learn Russian on your own was a near-impossible goal. However, he bought himself a teach-yourself-Russian primer and set about his task, which was not made any easier by his having to apply himself to Russian at the end of an already long day of study. Each evening, after supper, he would climb the spiral stairs at Ushaw Seminary on his way to his room, and each evening he would look into the recreation room as he passed, where his friends were relaxing, playing billiards, and chatting. Every time, he was tempted to join them and abandon his Russian. But evening after evening he resisted the temptation, climbed up to his room, and applied himself to acquiring that difficult language. Eventually, by about the time of his ordination, he had acquired a reading knowledge of it.

Soon after Gerald's ordination the war broke out and he volunteered to become an army chaplain. As a result, he shortly found himself in Beirut, Lebanon. There, to his great joy, he learned that there was a Russian community and that he would at last have an opportunity to exercise the language he had labored so long to learn. Unfortunately, to his utter dismay, he discovered that the Russians to whom he introduced himself did not understand a single word of his "Russian"—the sounds he had developed from the instructions in his teach-yourself book were wildly different from the sounds made by actual Russians! Still, the Russians in Beirut were kindly people, and over the next few months they taught him the correct sounds. Since he had mastered the grammar and a good deal of vocabulary it was not too long before he could conduct a conversation in the language.

The following year, Gerald was moved to Egypt and eventually went into the Western Desert with the Eighth Army. Once the battles against Rommel's forces began he was very busy, especially in the aftermath of battle when he comforted the wounded and dying. After one such engagement it was well beyond midnight before he felt he had done all he could for the soldiers in his care and could retire to his tent for the night.

Dead tired, he went into his tent where his batman was waiting. "Well, I think that's it for the night," said Gerald. But his batman replied, "No, padre. There's a fellow across in that tent who is dying. His guts are just about dropping out." So Gerald left his own tent and entered the one his batman had pointed out. There he found a man dying whom he had not seen before. He spoke to him in English, but received no reply, and in French, but again received no reply. One by one he tried all the languages he knew: Italian, German, Spanish, even Arabic. The dying man, however, made no response to any of them, and so it seemed that there was nothing Gerald could do, until slowly and painfully the man on the stretcher made the sign of the cross in the Russian Orthodox fashion.

"Are you Russian?" asked Gerald in Russian. When the man nodded, Gerald explained to him that Orthodox practice allowed him, as a Catholic priest, to hear his confession and give him absolution at this moment of his dying. The man was in no condition to make his formal confession, and Gerald, in any case, did not have sufficient mastery of Russian to lead him through it, but together they whispered the "Our Father" and Gerald gave him absolution. He held the man's hand until he died.

"When I came out of that tent in the early hours of the morning," Gerald said after telling me this story, "I suddenly remembered all those evenings when I would be climbing the spiral staircase at Ushaw; how I was tempted to give up my Russian and go into the recreation room. But in the darkness of that morning I said to myself, 'It was worth it, absolutely worth all that effort, just for this last hour with that dying man.'"

Responsible behavior at one moment in life may prove crucial many years later, in situations that no one could possibly have foreseen when the responsibility was first assumed.

I in turn feel that Gerald's story is worth telling, not simply in memory of him, but because it provides a memorable example of how responsible behavior at one moment in life may prove crucial many years later, in situations that no one could possibly have foreseen when the responsibility was first assumed.

The story also highlights what it means to describe our responsibility as total. It is total in the sense that in the name of holiness we have to assume responsibility for our past in much the same way as Jiyu Kennet did, and we have to assume responsibility for our future as Gerald Culkin did, or as the Edinburgh doctor failed to do. On the face of it these are very different tasks. We can know our past, but we cannot know our future. Essentially, however, the two tasks are not different, because although future events cannot be known and we cannot project into or plan for the future in any programmatic fashion, nevertheless each of us can assume responsibility for the all-important factor in our particular future, that is ourselves.

It is less important to *plan* what we shall do in different possible situations in the future than to *be* in our actual situation now. What will happen in the future we cannot know; but how we shall behave in that unknown future is determined by the kind of *be*ing that we are now, and for this we are totally responsible.

The *be*ing that each of us is supposed to be was discussed earlier in this chapter in terms of our total responsibility for our body. That emphasis, appropriate and necessary for a beginning, could prove misleading if we do not also recognize a complementary truth: it is not our bodies that are responsible. We are. And we are not our bodies. Nowhere has this complementary truth been more clearly manifested than in the life and teaching of the great Indian holy man of the twentieth century, Ramana Maharshi, who has indeed made it the very basis for his realization of holiness. In what a dramatic manner this came about has been told by Ramana Maharshi himself.

He was a healthy, vigorous lad of seventeen when one day quite suddenly a violent fear of death overtook him:

> The shock of the fear of death drove my mind inward and I said to myself mentally, without framing the words: "Now death has come; what does it mean? What is it that is dying? The body dies." And I at once dramatized the occurrence of death. I lay with my limbs stretched out stiff as though rigor mortis had set in and imitated a corpse so as to give greater reality to the enquiry. I held my breath and kept my lips tightly closed so that no sound could escape, so that neither the word "I" nor any other word could be uttered. "Well then," I said to myself, "this body is dead. It will be carried stiff to the burning ground and there burnt and reduced to ashes. But with the death of this body, am I dead? Is the body I? It is silent and inert but I feel the full force of my personality and even the voice of the 'I' within me, apart from it. So I am Spirit transcending the body. The body dies but the Spirit that transcends it cannot be touched by death. That means I am the deathless Spirit."[39]

This experiment by Ramana Maharshi is not quoted here in order to "prove" that man is a "deathless Spirit" (which it clearly does not do), but rather to show how one may realize that "I am not my body." All the same it is interesting to notice how closely it parallels the many accounts given by persons who came back after having been pronounced clinically dead. To quote just one such case, a doctor who had died in a motor accident recounts as follows:

---

39. A. Osborne, *The Teachings of Ramana Maharshi* (London, 1971), p. 10.

I saw my own dead body. I was surprised at the paleness of the face. I saw a number of persons sitting and standing about the body and particularly noticed two women apparently kneeling by my left side...I have since learned that they were my wife and my sister...I now attempted to gain the attention of the people but found that they gave me no heed. I concluded the matter by saying to myself: "They are watching what they think is I, but they are mistaken. That is not I. This is I and I am as much alive as ever."[40]

In the case of this doctor, as of Ramana Maharshi and other people who have realized that "I am not my body," the effect of the realization has been an all-pervading sense of peace and serenity. Some touch of that peace and serenity is accessible to all of us even if we are not granted the dramatic experiences recounted above.

It was under the simplest of circumstances, for instance, that I felt the touch of serenity and peace one morning. This happened a few moments after sunrise as I was kneeling on a newly-mown lawn making my morning meditation. The warmth of the sun seemed to animate lots of small flies and gnats that had settled in the grass, and they swarmed around my bare forearms, resting upon my thighs. Seemingly in celebration of the brilliant sun's rays, many of them settled now upon the skin of my arms and thighs, taking them over, occupying them. The earnestness of their occupation made me smile, and forced me to acknowledge to them that my body was for the moment on loan to them.

---

40. J. C. Hampe, *To Die Is Gain* (London, 1979), p. 38.

And then, in the joy of that sharing, I also realized that this body, this incredibly delicate composition, was equally on loan to me. "My" body is not me. It is on loan, and from a higher source than either the body or me; and at any moment I may be called upon to return it to that higher source. This realization in no way makes me feel alienated from my body. On the contrary, because I do not make a fierce, possessive identification with it but occupy it peacefully, I feel a deep, tender care toward it. Now I know that I must not ill-treat my body in the name of pleasure, or ambition, or competition, or science. The only cause in which I may properly surrender it is in the name of that higher source of both the body and myself, the Holy One. When I remember that I belong to this source I feel the touch of serenity and peace.

The only cause in which I may properly surrender my body is in the name of that higher source of both the body and myself, the Holy One.

Perhaps it seems odd to emphasize this feeling of serenity and peace when the theme of this chapter has been responsibility, and the very word "responsibility" normally connotes some heavy charge laid upon us for which we shall be punished unless we discharge our obligation correctly. But to accept such a connotation is to be stuck at a very superficial level of responsibility. After all, the word itself should prompt us to penetrate more deeply, since "responsibility" arises out of "response" and there can only be response if there is a call. If there is a call, there is a caller, and the ultimate caller is the Holy One, calling us to holiness.

Certainly a note is heard in that call which daunts us—*terribilis est locus iste,* as Jacob exclaimed at Bethel, "awesome is this place"—for once the caller awakens us out of our sleep, we are struck by a terrible realization of what it means to be a human being, what awful consequences our actions may bear both for ourselves and for other beings. However, if we listen faithfully there is a much deeper and more sustained note in the voice of the caller, which is the note of longing on the part of the Holy One that each of us may share in this travail of creation. The voice is assuring us of the wonderful consequences both for ourselves and for all creation if only we will respond generously and faithfully to the call. Responsibility is awesome, true, but it is also tremendously bracing. It is when neither the awesome nor the bracing is denied that one feels the touch of serenity and peace.

That touch is in no way an impersonal one like the touch of a steering wheel or of a piece of pottery; it is the warm touch of One who is reaching toward us out of longing that we also should be holy. The personal quality of this touch is often brought home to us by studying the lives of those who have themselves responded to it positively— warmly and in complete generosity—that is, the saints. But sometimes it is through observing a negative reaction, a refusal to respond, that one is shaken into recognizing the personal nature of the touch and the personal sadness inflicted by that refusal. Lately an English writer has described such negation—his own negation, in fact. He writes of it as a curious episode.... I had a religious experience. It took place in the Church of San Lorenzo, but it did not seem to be connected with the harmonious beauty of the architecture. I can only say that for a few minutes my whole being was irradiated by a kind of heavenly joy, far more intense than anything I had known before. This state of mind lasted for several months, and wonderful though it was, it posed an awkward problem in terms of action. My life was far from blameless: I would have to reform. My family would think I was going mad, and perhaps after all it was a delusion, for I was in every way unworthy of receiving such a flood of grace. Gradually the effect wore off, and I made no effort to retain it. I think I was right: I was too deeply embedded in the world to change course. But that I had "felt the finger of God" I am quite sure, and, although the memory of this experience has faded, it still helps me to understand the joys of the saints.[41]

Who could read that passage without hearing beneath its words an echo of the voice of the Holy One calling the writer of the passage? Who could fail to see that the very recalling of the episode, after so many years, is a sign that the Holy One is still calling to the writer if only he will respond, become responsible, and re-form his life? It reminds us that the Holy One was longing for each of us to be holy before ever we began to do so, and that he continues to do so even when we ourselves get tired of our longing. The way in which we respond to that personal call is our total responsibility.

41. K. Clark, *The Other Half: A Self-Portrait* (London, 1977), p. 108.

6

Stop: Be Still

HOW A PERSON DRIVES A CAR IS OFTEN A GOOD INDICATION OF whether or not he or she has begun to assume responsibility for his or her actions. And there is no surer sign of irresponsibility than to drive a car without knowing how to stop it. In fact, the first thing one needs to know about a car, or any machine for that matter, is how to stop it. The same applies to the traffic of our daily lives. Unless we can stop the rush and noise of daily traffic in our lives, we do not have the slightest chance of hearing the call to holiness. As was pointed out at the beginning of the previous two chapters, the practice those chapters describe is perfectly simple. The same is true of this practice. There, Rabi'a's prescription for patience was, "stop complaining." The prescription for this chapter is, "stop, before you try to go any further."

Is the reader of these lines, or the author of them, capable of stopping? The reader can test herself or himself, as did the author. Having recognized for times without number that in holiness practice is everything and words are nothing, I stopped at that point. Let the reader do the same—stop, and do nothing for ten minutes, sitting perfectly still. Sometimes the attempt to do no more than that may prove quite humiliating; one discovers that one has taken so little responsibility for one's own body over the course of the years that not even for ten minutes can one keep it from moving around restlessly.

Stopping one's body from squirming around may seem a trivial exercise, but in fact it is not a trivial matter, any more than the skill to stop one's car is a trivial part of being a consummate driver. There are superior and more spectacular skills for a driver than stopping his car, but none of them is of any use without that basic skill. The same is true of the ability to stop one's bodily movements and to be still. Indeed some Zen Buddhists maintain that sitting still, or *zazen,* as they call it, is not only the beginning of enlightenment practice, but also the end. When you can sit perfectly you are perfectly enlightened. Of course, there is more to this aphorism than meets the eye; if sitting were the only thing, then, as one Zen master observed, toads would have achieved enlightenment.

Nevertheless it is true that the simple act of trying to sit still can prove a real revelation to the sitter as to his or her state of being. Above all, a person who is doing *zazen* and then finds him or herself starting to get angry, or frustrated, or restless for no apparent reason is thereby made to realize that no external event or agent is producing this condition in him. No one has done anything whatsoever. That person has just been sitting, alone, so that person is responsible for whatever anger, frustration or restlessness is experienced.

What the attempt to stop and be still reveals to most people is that they are in a hurry; they are ahead of themselves, incapable of resting on one spot. As Pascal has said, "All the miseries of mankind arise from man's inability to sit still in his own room." Indeed, Muslim tradition goes so far as to define man as the being who is always ahead of himself, toppling forward off balance in trying to catch up with himself.

How often we use that phrase, "Once I've caught up with myself," without recognizing the absurdity of our position! Who is the self that has run ahead? And who is the "I" that has been left behind? Once again a simple experiment will provide some answer. Stop reading. Then realize the possibility that you will never leave the room where you now are alive—the place where you are now sitting, or lying down, or standing is the last place you will ever occupy on this earth. If you do manage to stop, you will be led to realize through your imagination that your self has already run outside the room into some other place and some other time, restless on account of desires and worries and plans. Yet those desires and worries and plans are all in vain, because you will never leave the room in

> **What the attempt to stop and be still reveals to most people is that they are in a hurry; they are ahead of themselves, incapable of resting on one spot.**

which you now find yourself. In fact, in order to find yourself, the worst thing you could do is to start trying to catch
up with those desires, worries, and plans.

The only thing to do is to sit still and become collected;
when you do so, then all the bits of yourself that had
become scattered outside the room in desires, worries, and
plans will gradually be drawn back to you and you will be
collected—you will have found yourself.

Very strikingly and succinctly, the Indian holy man
Meher Baba has epitomized this teaching. He said, "Mind
racing—madman; mind quiet—saint; mind still—God."
And while Meher Baba was speaking immediately about
the mind, it has to be remembered that the quieting of the
mind can begin with a stilling of the body.

This was wonderfully illustrated by the story of Dr. E.
F. Schumacher, author of *Small Is Beautiful.* Schumacher
tells how, into his middle years, he was a conventional
Western intellectual, agnostic and rudderless, as well as
being economic adviser to a number of countries, among
them Burma (now Myanmar), which had impressed him
specially because its ordinary people seemed to carry
around with them such an air of calmness. Aware of the
Burmese practice by which a large proportion of the people
spend some considerable time in their Buddhist monaster-
ies, Schumacher himself arranged to spend several weeks
in a monastery observing the discipline. So he went and sat
for about five weeks, learning to be still.

Those five weeks proved to be the turning point of his
life. Gradually his body became still; and then, as his
desires stopped running away with him, his heart became

quiet; and finally, as a result, his mind became clear.[42] It was this resultant clarity of mind which more than anything surprised Dr. Schumacher. As a gifted, highly trained intellectual, he had always supposed himself to be clear-minded, whereas he now realized that in the past his mind had been obscured by the ever-shifting clouds of his restless desires. This hitherto unknown clarity of mind enabled him to tread surely on the spiritual path that now revealed itself to him and to become one of the genuine prophets of the twentieth century.

Yet it is hardly surprising that we cannot see any realities clearly—least of all, spiritual realities—if we are being rapidly whisked along by our desires. We need only to reflect on how difficult it is to see anything clearly when we are being whisked along in an express train or a fast car. One telegraph pole flashes past just as we are beginning to focus on the last one; our attention is caught by a tree and we begin to examine what kind of a tree it is when, in an instant, it vanishes and we never know what kind it was. Sometimes, indeed, if our driver is in a tremendous hurry, we cannot even tell whether it was a telegraph pole or a tree that flashed past.

A truly terrifying example of how hurry can blind us to reality has been given in an experiment carried out by a group of American psychologists. They took a class of young theological students, settled them in a room at one end of a large hospital, and then told them that they were taking part in an experiment in verbal retention. Each of

---

42. E. F. Schumacher, "Buddhist Economics" in *Small Is Beautiful* (London, 1974), pp. 51–60.

the students would be asked individually to go into a room where a psychologist would read a passage to him, and the student would then be sent down the long corridor to the other end of the hospital where he would be asked to repeat what he had heard. His words would be recorded and his verbal retention would be measured by comparing his words with the original passage.

In fact, the psychologists had other aims in mind than testing the students' verbal retention. To half of the students they read a variety of passages, but they read the Parable of the Good Samaritan to all the others; and they stationed a man in a shallow alcove halfway along the corridor and had him lie upon the ground, battered-looking like the man in the parable. The psychologists were intent upon discovering whether the percentage of those who stopped to help the battered-looking man increased among those who had heard the parable as compared with those who had heard quite a different passage.

Hurry blinds us.

They discovered that the number of students who stopped to help the battered-looking man was not high and was not appreciably higher among those who had heard the parable than among those who had not. But equally significant was the fact that certain students in the former group had been told by the psychologists, after having heard the parable, to *hurry* along to the other end of the corridor. And not a single one of them had stopped to help the battered-looking man! They seem not even to have noticed him. Hurry blinds us.

By contrast, whenever we are still, all beings stand out distinctively in their own individuality, revealing their intricate beauty and splendor and prompting us spontaneously to utter a song of praise for the creator of such beauty and splendor. Knowing how essential stillness is for seeing this beauty and splendor, I once asked each member of a class on mysticism to go into the redwoods and make note of any particular tree that for some reason caught their attention. For the rest of the term they were to go once a week to that particular redwood, sit beside it in silence, and simply observe it, taking in its individuality.

Needless to say some students found this assignment extremely taxing; they were conditioned to believe that you cannot be learning unless a professor is talking to you. But many others found the discipline very revealing; everything about that spot—the snails, the blades of grass, the dewdrops as well as the redwood—began to stand out, each thing in its glorious individuality.

This experience of stillness and patience made a profound impression upon them. By way of contrast, one remembers the remark of a Californian politician that "when you have seen one redwood you have seen them all." Not surprisingly, that politician came from a city notorious for fast cars, fast films, fast food, and mindless whirl.

The truth we are here considering has been summed up forever in the Psalms (46:10), where we are commanded, "Be still and know that I am God." [43] It is in stillness,

---

43. This is the usual translation. Literally it means "stop" as in the heading for this chapter.

in silence, that we know God. For in the Semitic world to which the Psalmist belonged, stillness and silence were recognized to be two facets of the same reality. It is fascinating, for instance, to learn that the Hebrew word for the presence of God, *shekinah,* has the same root as the Arabic word for that pause, or silence, which a pious Muslim observes at one point in the prostrations made during the course of the prayers prayed five times each day. This Arabic word is *sukun.* So the Jew and the Muslim are at one in the conviction that it is in silence, in stillness, that God comes to dwell among us, to be present to us, and to transfigure us, as Jesus was transfigured on Mount Tabor.

This discipline of silence is cultivated in every religious tradition. In the Christian tradition those who made a special virtue out of silence were called *hesychasts,* from the Greek word *hesychia,* meaning quietness. In the Hindu tradition they are called *muni,* a title derived from a Sanskrit word that means "to shut"—in this context literally keeping one's mouth shut, never saying anything.

One such *muni* of my acquaintance, Baba Hari Dass, has not spoken now for over a quarter of a century, though he does at times communicate his penetrating thoughts by writing on a chalkboard. When I asked him what was the effect of living under a vow of silence, he replied that it soon made you realize how easily and frequently human beings speak for no good reason but simply as a means of indulging their egotism. Soon after a *muni* has taken his vow, for example, he will find himself listening to a conversation and will feel the impulse to intervene and then realize that by virtue of his vow he cannot do so.

Once he realizes this, he is able, in a detached fashion, to examine objectively the impulse that had moved him to want to speak. He is frequently amazed to see that this impulse was not rooted in a desire to dispel ignorance or to calm the anger of those participating in the conversation, as he had imagined. It was rooted in vanity, in a desire to show off his learning, or wisdom, or nobility, or great suffering—in any case to display his own ego.

A further effect of this vow of silence is that the *muni* develops tremendous patience and tolerance. He often has to be present when people are talking nonsense and laying down the law on subjects of which they are ignorant and in which he is expert, yet he cannot intervene by word of mouth. Day in and day out this restraint breeds the rarest patience. At the same time it makes him face the only way that is open to him to bring the participants to recognize their own ignorance and vanity. That way is the way that God also works, by his very presence through silence, through the *shekinah,* the dwelling among men.

By choosing silence the *muni* is, as it were, compelled to abandon the naturally egotistic, forceful, speedy way of trying to influence people in preference for a spiritual, gentle, and slow way of permeating them with his presence. He comes to recognize "that one's relations with people are to a large extent at the level of the subconscious. Vague hints and intuitions reinforce the feelings we have about people that they are either good or bad."

Those words are the words used by Fosco Maraini when he was trying to describe the lesson he had learned from a silent Tibetan lama. Maraini goes on to say of him: "Lama

Tendav emanates peace and benevolence almost as though they were physical realities; he radiates an inner light."[44]

Virtually the same words are used by Sanjiva Rao to describe what happened to him when he went to Anandamayi, a modern Indian holy woman. After he had unburdened himself to her of the agonizing problem that he was facing, "she spoke no word, offered no verbal explanation. Yet within a couple of minutes my mind was in a state of deep stillness; the problem was effortlessly dissolved—I was in a state of ineffable peace and joy."[45]

An similar incident, but even more remarkable, is related of St. Seraphim of Sarov, the Russian "saint of silence" who spent some thirty years as a hermit in the great forest of Temniki. On one occasion a student from Kiev, 400 miles away, being troubled by a spiritual conflict and having heard of Seraphim's holiness, set off to walk all the way to the monastery of Sarov and seek the holy hermit's advice. When eventually the student arrived at the monastery and inquired for Father Seraphim, he was directed to Seraphim's hermitage, several miles beyond the monastery in the thick forest. After walking for over an hour, the student came to a clearing in which he saw Seraphim's hut, but there was no sign of Seraphim himself.

Then he noticed the hermit curled up like a squirrel in the thick grass, sleeping after his work in his vegetable garden. For a long time the student simply stood and gazed at the sleeping holy man. As he did so a great peace came upon him; the spiritual conflict that had brought him all the

---

44. Fosco Mariani, *Secret Tibet* (London, 1952), p. 201.
45. Sanjiva Rao, *Ma Anandamayi* (Calcutta, 1973), p. 69.

way to Sarov was resolved; and without even waking
Seraphim or exchanging a word with him, the student set
off straightaway to walk the 400 miles back to Kiev! A holy
man who has learned, through silence, to speak without
words, can resolve spiritual conflicts even in his sleep.

"Silence," said Seraphim, "is the cross on which man
must crucify his ego"; "silence transfigures a man into an
angel; it is the spiritual practice which most surely pre-
serves inner peace." He was constantly repeating the words
of St. Ambrose: "I have seen many who were saved by
silence but none who were saved by chatter."[46]

Of course St. Seraphim, Baba Hari Dass, and Anandamayi are instances of very special vocations. Few of us
can take vows of silence such as theirs. But this does not
mean to say that we cannot follow the discipline perfectly
in accordance with our own calling.

Take the story, for instance, of the rabbi whom Reb
Aryeh went to visit. This extraordinarily learned rabbi
had published three great volumes of rabbinical teaching
entirely devoted to analyzing the varied sins of the tongue.
Since the learned man was so aware of the sins of the
tongue that he needed three volumes to analyze them, Reb
Aryeh anticipated that when he met him the man would
prove to be very grave and silent, a man of few, ponderous
words. To his surprise and delight, when they met the
learned rabbi kept up a pleasant and lively conversation all
the time, yet without the least shadow of sin! Through a
long discipline the rabbi had learned to ensure that his

46. V. Zander, *Seraphim von Sarov* (Düsseldorf, 1965) p. 41.

words arose out of that silence, the *shekinah,* which is the presence of God; they did not arise out of the verbiage that is a sign of man's egotism.

Verbiage is the mark of a person who is full of himself. There is no room in him for God because such a person is already full, preoccupied with himself and his own opinions. That preoccupation, according to many Buddhist teachers, is the main obstacle that prevents their Western pupils from achieving enlightenment: "They are so full of opinions on everything; and so they never come to know anything."

The remedy for verbiage (the symptom of opinions) is obviously to empty oneself of one's preoccupations. One of the nicest remarks ever made on the subject of preoccupation was by Robert Speaight when speaking of Hilaire Belloc's rage against Edwardian plutocrats. Speaight said, "Belloc was no doubt right about the Edwardian plutocrats, but he ought never to have allowed them so much room in his mind."

Discrimination regarding who or what we allow to have room in our minds, to preoccupy us, can only be achieved if we regularly empty our minds of our preoccupations. Emptiness, stillness, silence—each of these words is an attempt to pinpoint the condition in which God is known. In a daring passage, the author of the Letter to the Philippians proposes Jesus as the model from whom we have to learn this self-emptying: "Let this mind be in you which was also in Christ Jesus who, though he was God, did not cling on to his equality with God but emptied himself and took upon himself the form of a servant."[47]

---

47. Philippians 2:5–7.

The utter grace with which Jesus accomplished this self-emptying should not delude us into imagining that we can easily do the same. Most of us have no chance of doing so unless we honestly acknowledge how full we are with our own preoccupations, and how tenaciously we cling to them.

The remedy for verbiage (the symptom of opinions) is obviously to empty oneself of one's preoccupations

An extraordinarily apt illustration of this was once provided for me by a friend. I had been remarking on how frequently in medieval hagiography one comes across stories in which people fail to recognize the holy one because their minds are already made up, preoccupied by their own conception of what the holy one should be like. Such a story will tell, for instance, about a knight who sets off on a journey to receive the blessing of a holy abbot named Guido, and as he draws near to the holy abbot's monastery he sees a small, grizzled fellow toiling amid the furrows of the monastery fields. "Where," the knight haughtily asks, "can I find Abbot Guido?" In reply, the small, grizzled fellow points out to him the path to the monastery. In arriving at the monastery the knight is reverently greeted by the guest master and again puts forward his request to see the holy abbot. The guest master says he will bring him along shortly and then asks their distinguished guest to take a seat.

A few minutes later the guest master returns in the company of the holy abbot who turns out—much to the knight's astonishment—to be none other than the small, grizzled fellow whom he had met toiling in the fields.

"That is nothing," said my friend. "I once went to a Greek island specially in order to see a *starets* (a holy monk). I was well received at the monastery where the *starets* lived and was given a cell to occupy during my stay on the island. The next day, I was reading a life of a medieval Greek saint, which contained several stories of precisely the kind you have just described. I was absorbed in the book when there was a knock on the cell door and a wiry, bright-eyed little monk put his head round the door to ask me if I would like to go for a walk with him.

"Since I was so preoccupied with my book I thanked him and said that I was studying at the moment but would like to walk with him later. About an hour afterward there was again a knock on the door and once more the wiry, bright-eyed little monk was there, asking me if I would like to go for a walk. I was slightly irritated, and just on the point of excusing myself for a second time when I remembered the stories I had been reading. Sure enough, the wiry, bright-eyed little monk was the very *starets* I had come all this way to see! I had turned him away once and had almost turned him away a second time—even though at that very moment I was reading stories that were all about failing to see the holy one you are searching for when he actually appears!"

Preoccupation instead of emptiness; restlessness instead of stillness; noise instead of silence; hurtling along unable to stop: all of these render us incapable of noticing the battered man on the roadside, of seeing the holy man we are searching for, or hearing the call of longing from the Holy One. The cause of all these failures can be summed up in one word: "hurry." As far as I am concerned, this point can hardly be overemphasized, as I have often reflected that almost every wrong I have ever committed in the course of my life has resulted from being in a hurry. And as if to underline the insidiousness of hurry, at the very moment I wrote those words of caution against hurry I was in danger of once more toppling over into hurry in my desire to finish writing this chapter by a certain date.

Why are we almost always in a hurry? If only we can answer that question we may then learn how to slow down, even to stop, be still, and know God. The main difficulty in answering the question lies in our tendency to give self-excusing, dishonest answers by painting our fundamental vices as virtues. Almost always, for instance, when you ask a middle-class English person how he is he replies, "Very busy," which, in an oblique manner, is a way of telling you that he is in a hurry and therefore does not have much time for you. But people regard this busy-ness not as a fault but as a virtue, since they are letting you know that they are engaged in many virtuous tasks, such as building a career or making a garden or saving someone's soul.

However, the honest answer to the question of why we are almost always in a hurry is much simpler. In one word, it is greed. Greed may take many forms. Often, of course, it takes the simple form of greed for food or for sexual satisfaction. On other occasions it is greed for experience, whether of travel or of music or of culture in general; sometimes it takes the form of greed for information or, equally often, for flattery. But whatever form it takes, greed generates hurry by leading us to try to push in more than there is really room or time for—literally in the primitive case of food, or figuratively in the case of culture and information.

Once again it is best to begin at the basic level of food in order to understand how this happens. Notice, when you are eating, whether you pick up one morsel of food, either by hand or by fork, before you have actually swallowed the previous morsel. If you find that you do, then make a point of putting down your fork or folding your hands in between morsels; the measure of the awkwardness you feel in doing so is the measure of your greed and, therefore, of your hurry.

A nice story to illustrate this point is told of Thich Nhat Hanh. During the Vietnam war he was traveling around the United States with James Douglas to explain the Vietnamese viewpoint to American audiences. One day they chose to sit under a tree to eat their lunch. After lunch Thich Nhat Hanh said to his companion, "James, I must teach you how to eat an orange." "But I have just eaten one," replied Douglas. "I don't think you did eat it," said Thich Nhat Hanh. "I noticed that after you had peeled the orange you placed one segment of it into your mouth and immediately took another segment into your hand before swallowing the first one. And when you placed the second segment in your mouth you immediately seized a third one. All the time your mind was upon the next segment; so, in any real sense you never ate any of it. You were in such a hurry to eat the whole of the orange that you never actually ate a single segment of it."

In regard to food and sex, most of us are probably prepared to recognize, even though grudgingly, that greed is a
source of hurry for us. In regard to other, more "elevated"
matters we are far more reluctant to do so. While gulping
food or wallowing in sex may still be frowned on—at least
in certain old-fashioned circles—as a gross form of behavior, even those old-fashioned circles tend to regard wallowing in music or swallowing culture as virtues, and therefore
in no sense as forms of greed that engender hurry and constitute obstacles to holiness. How such "elevated" matters
can prove the subtlest of all forms of greed may be illustrated by an example.

Some years ago I took it upon myself to keep informed
on all aspects of modern life and thought (to "stuff myself
with opinions," as one of our Buddhist masters might say).
On the face of it this is a most laudable undertaking, and
that is certainly how I thought of it at the time.
Consequently I read endless books on political affairs, tech-
nological advances, philosophical analysis, spirituality,
anthropology, and so on—endlessly. And at the same time
I subscribed to journals and periodicals in many languages
dealing with the same subjects—which in effect meant
everything under the sun.

The undertaking was an exciting one, especially at the
beginning. It was immensely stimulating, like a new drug,
and, as with a drug, gave me the feeling that I was now seeing connections that I had never seen before. Soon, however, the excitement began to wear off and the stimulation
began to give way before a gnawing sense of always being
behind. As the books and journals continued to pile up and

as my notes and observations upon them continued to grow, I was continually trying to catch up with myself (my "self," of course, perpetually receding ever faster into the growing piles). But no matter how fast I read, no matter how late into the night I worked or how early I got up in the morning, I never seemed to get any nearer to "catching up with myself."

The absurdity of my behavior is now epitomized for me in my memory by an image from that period of myself at breakfast. Before going to work in the morning I would be eating my breakfast at the same time I was reading the newspaper while also trying to listen to news and commentary from the radio! There was no Sabbath in that life, none of the peace that comes from putting a stop to the endless hurry to catch up.

However, since I chose not to accord my system a Sabbath, not unnaturally my system decided to go on strike. My body went in for a breakdown. During the rest that had been forced upon me, I was able to see with complete clarity that my desire for information was just another form of greed, more "elevated" if you like than lust for a juicy steak or a juicy blonde, but greed nonetheless. I was just as much hooked on information as a person who is on drugs, such as alcohol, nicotine, cocaine, or coffee. Anything to which you are so attached that you cannot say, "No. Stop."—even information, or music, or painting, or theater—is a drug; it is out of control and sweeping you along with it in its mad career.

The term "drug" is, in fact, a most appropriate one since it prompts us to recognize how hurry and noise and greed are inextricably intertwined. It focuses our attention on the loss of control and the abdication of responsibility that go hand in hand with addiction. It is worth remembering that at its root the word "addiction" is derived from Roman law and originally meant "to deliver over formally by judicial sentence." It then came to mean, "attached to one's own act," to some object or pursuit, such as cocaine or culture, which enslaves or divests you of responsibility (which is the same thing). Since any such attachment or addiction is a kind of drug, the way of becoming detached and liberated has to be very similar to the way in which drug addicts are cured. First, and most important, the drug addict has to acknowledge fully that he or she is, in fact, an addict. This in its turn can only happen if he or she can stand back and cease to identify the self with the illusion of the drug—in other words, by detachment. Second, that person has to recognize that he or she can only be cured by calling upon some source of power other than the addicted self—in other words, by meditation and prayer.

Anything to which you are so attached that you cannot say, "No. Stop."— even information, or music, or painting, or theater—is a drug; it is out of control and sweeping you along with it in its mad career.

The practice of detachment is actually a way of learning how to respond to events or persons instead of reacting to them. This fundamental distinction between reacting and responding can be appreciated from all sorts of experiences. When someone, for instance, offends one of our deeply ingrained prejudices, we tend to react instantly, almost mechanically, like a puppet; anyone acquainted with us will be able virtually to predict our "knee-jerk" reaction. But if we have been schooling ourselves to respond rather than to react, when our prejudices are touched upon we will be able to insert a stop, a pause *(sukun),* which establishes a distance between the event and ourselves, an interval in which we have the opportunity to exercise our personal freedom by choosing how we shall respond to this assault upon our prejudices.

When we react we are behaving mechanically; when we respond we are exercising our freedom, behaving responsibly. When we react our whole being is centered upon our ego; our ego occupies the whole of our universe—there is nothing else for us in that instant outside that egotistic universe. When we respond, on the other hand, we take into consideration much more than our own ego; the pause gives us space to open our hearts to all creatures—including the one who is assaulting our prejudices—and in that sense we assume responsibility, implicitly at least, for the whole of the universe.

From what has just been said, it is clear that the cultivation of responsiveness and the cutting down of reaction is actually an exercise in detachment. The interval which responsiveness allows for the development of responsibility at the same time enables us to see beyond the end of our own noses. We then have to make an acknowledgement that is always hard to make—the acknowledgment that we really are hooked on our prejudices or our drugs. Fortunately, there enters a wonderful balancing truth: as soon as we begin to acknowledge honestly that we are hooked, then the hook immediately begins to detach itself. Since we can now see that our ego has been mechanically attached to a particular drug and we have identified ourselves with it, we can also recognize that our seeing heart has freed us from that identification. Once we can no longer call our prejudices "our own," we are detached from them, liberated from them.

Since every being or thought or quality can be turned into an object of addiction ("God" included), it is obviously impossible to list all the objects from which one has to detach oneself. However, as this chapter has been much concerned with realizing how hurry constitutes an obstacle to holiness, at least a word or two seems in order about our relationship with time, especially since human beings have always had an obscure awareness that that relationship can easily become a cause of enslavement and addiction. The communards of Paris in 1870, for instance, bore witness to that awareness when, for a start to their revolution, they went around Paris shooting off the arms of all the public clocks because the clock was an agent of their enslavement. They agreed with the traditional saying of the Hasidim, "Where there is a clock, there is no soul."

Once the obscure awareness of our relationship with time as a potential cause of enslavement and addiction is transformed into a clear recognition of why that is so, we can then see the root of our addiction and root it out. Surely it happens because we regard time as "our own," as though it were our private property that we have to defend. Witness how often we use the phrase "my time," humorlessly claiming as our own a few seconds or a few hours out of all those millions of light years that came before us and that will come after us. Notice how we hurry to the defense of "my time" as if it were our private property. Hurry is actually a form of violence exercised upon God's time in order to make it "my time."

Consider, for instance, the everyday and seemingly trivial example of signing a letter or a check. How often the signatures on such documents are illegible because the signatory was in such a hurry that he or she produced a veritable squiggle that someone else had to spend much time deciphering. The signatory's hurry was a sort of violence by which someone else's time is taken up. Such an instance is only seemingly trivial because, in fact, it is the small, everyday incidents that often reveal most clearly our condition. This statement carries the heartening corollary that by seemingly trivial actions one can begin to remedy one's condition.

Take the case we have cited, for instance, of signing a document. Once you have realized how your signature reveals your hurried condition, all you need do, every time you notice yourself writing hurriedly, is to start writing carefully and slowly instead. That small action, if regularly practiced, will have a transforming effect: gradually you will slow down, become calmer and more collected. Not only that, but the change in your condition will produce a change in how you perceive things; you will cease to think of time as your own to be violently defended and realize that time is a gift common to all creatures and has to be shared.

Slowing down one's hurried signature is one possible way some people may detach themselves from the rush of time, but the classical manner of teaching human beings detachment from slavery or addiction to time is the institution of the day of rest, traditionally called the Sabbath. It is still good to use the term "Sabbath" because even though days of rest may be observed by humanity in general, it is the Jewish people, more than any other, which has preserved the Sabbath and has itself been preserved by that observance.

How vital the Sabbath is to them is reflected in a humorous Hasidic anecdote. It concerns a Jewish trader who so grossly overloaded the wagon on which he was to transport his merchandise that his horses could not pull it. He thought of lightening the load by taking off some of the merchandise, but later decided against doing so—because he felt that each item was indispensable to his career. Still, something had to go; so he took the wheels off his wagon! You do the same when you dispense with the Sabbath.

Unfortunately, many Westerners who foolishly wish to imitate the Jewish trader and justify taking the wheels off their wagon have at hand a scriptural quotation that they glibly produce. They say, with an air of wisdom, "But the Sabbath was made for man, and not man for the Sabbath." They misguidedly imagine that the quotation means that it is up to them to decide how they will use "their time" on the Sabbath. Whereas, in fact, the scriptural quotation means the opposite: that the Sabbath is precisely God's time, a pause *(sukun)* for our sake, decided upon by God, a period when we must stop working, worrying, and planning, when we must let go all of those activities and, instead, be still, simply rejoicing in the presence of God *(shekinah)*.

The fact that so many people pervert the scriptural quotation about the Sabbath, making it mean the opposite of what it says, only indicates how deeply resistant we are to accepting the lesson that the institution of the Sabbath is intended to teach—and how very firm and strict one has to be with oneself, therefore, in observing the Sabbath discipline.

Quite simply, Sabbath discipline requires that at a fixed and definite moment on a fixed day each week one stops working—not on any day one chooses, nor at any moment one chooses, but precisely when God says, because only God knows how very prone human beings are to give themselves excuses and make exceptions for themselves in face of Sabbath discipline. Anyone who has not been brought up observing the Sabbath can testify to the difficulty of starting to do so faithfully: always, it seems, there is still some little job that has to be finished, which cannot be finished before the Sabbath begins. Always, it seems, there is some tremendously responsible undertaking next week, for which one will be inadequately prepared unless one does a certain amount of work on the Sabbath. If one pays heed to these considerations, the fact is that one will never observe the Sabbath; one will never say "stop" and put a stop to the hurry of daily life.

The only thing to do is quite firmly to stop working at the appointed time and be still, to empty one's mind of the worries and plans connected with work. Even though some tremendous undertaking may be on your program for next week, and for which you feel inadequately prepared, do not so much as think about it. As soon as the thought of a program for the future comes into your mind, dismiss it. The best preparation for any undertaking whatsoever is being at peace with God.

The best preparation for any undertaking whatsoever is being at peace with God.

As with all forms of liberation by way of detachment, so with the Sabbath; the way at first, from outside, seems daunting and austere. Anything to which you are so attached that you cannot say, "No. Stop."—even information, or music, or painting, or theater—is a drug; it is out of control and sweeping you along with it in its mad career.

This happens imperceptibly: the knowledge that you will not be working on the Sabbath means that you have to order the rest of your week differently. Like the Jewish trader who overloaded his wagon, you have to get rid of some of your load. You then discover, as he would have discovered if only he had not dispensed with the Sabbath, that much of what you have been carrying is superfluous; you are now much lighter and can move with an easy rhythm. Something of the stillness, peace, and joy of the Sabbath has begun to permeate all of your days. Where the Sabbath at one time appeared to be forbidding, an interruption of your good and necessary work, now it is seen to be quite the reverse. You now experience the rest of the week as a preparation for the peace and joy of the Sabbath, and the process of preparation itself permeates the whole week with the fragrance of the Sabbath. A rhythm has now been established in your life that means that you can stop when necessary and you can also move easily when necessary.

"It is by doing the truth," says St. John the Evangelist, "that you come to the light,"[48] you become enlightened; and it is by doing the Sabbath, by following its commands, that you learn the lesson it is meant to teach. The lesson is that "our time" is not really our time at all; that is sheer illusion. We cannot own time; it is not our own. Only by sharing time does it become a reality for us, instead of an illusion to which we are addicted.

In the immediately preceding paragraphs we have used the Sabbath as an example of how we may work toward detachment from one of the most common human addictions, the addiction to "my time." But the fact that any being, thought, and quality can be turned into an object of addiction by the human mind means that we should never be under the illusion that we are altogether detached.

A rather frightening warning on this score has been given to us by that great teacher of detachment, St. John of the Cross. After listing the many and subtle ways in which we become attached, St. John of the Cross goes on to say that no matter how seemingly slight an attachment may be, if we fail to break it, we remain enslaved. In a famous image he compares the human soul to a bird that wants to soar into God's heaven. The bird may indeed have escaped

---

48. John 3:21.

from the cage of sensual attachments and may no longer be chained to the ground by heavy chains of human respect; nevertheless it still has tied around its leg the slenderest of silken threads, representing attachment to spiritual consolations. No matter that the attachment is fine and slender: unless that final thread is broken, the bird, or the soul, can no more soar into God's heaven than if it were held down by a gross iron chain.[49]

Properly understood, of course, this famous image carries a salutary message: any attachment, however slight, is still a potential source of addiction or enslavement. A person may, for instance, be in the habit of occupying the same seat each day on a bus or in a church or at a table. A matter of very slight importance, one may think; and yet if the person finds himself disturbed and upset on the odd occasions when another person is occupying the chair, then that is a warning sign. People have been known to get so unbalanced over such matters that they have quarreled, and even become life-long enemies.

However, in the past this image of the silken thread has been invoked in such a way as to give rise to serious misunderstanding through literal interpretation. Many people have been discouraged by it, taking it to mean that unless you can achieve total detachment, there is not much point in struggling against any particular attachments. The obvious falsity of this interpretation drives us, by way of opposition, to recognize yet another salutary truth: none of us will ever be totally detached this side of death. We need

---

49. St. John of the Cross, *Complete Works,* vol. I, p. 53.

only think of St. John of the Cross himself in his last days; during that time he asked to be given spinach to eat, a food for which he had a special liking. And it is interesting to remember that St. Francis of Assisi and St. Thomas Aquinas expressed similar desires for special food on their deathbeds. St. Francis asked for Lady Jacopa Giacoma to bring him some marzipan. St. Thomas Aquinas requested his companions to grill for him a particular kind of fish that was a specialty of the region.

I cite these examples not in order to show that even the greatest saints suffered from the same weaknesses as the rest of us, but rather that no one should be discouraged by imagining that it is no good achieving detachment from anything unless you can snap the last silken thread.

The image of the silken thread tied to the bird's leg must fade in the face of the truth that every time anyone breaks an attachment, a fresh source of joy opens up in that person, and the more attachments that are broken the deeper and wider that joy becomes. One reason for the increase in joy is that the person is now less and less easily disturbed; being addicted to fewer and fewer things or persons means that there are fewer and fewer occasions when things are taken away, or when persons let one down; so one is not so often disturbed, one is better balanced. With better balance a person becomes more centered, so that joy and peace and serenity are able to sink ever deeper into one's being, until eventually they touch the person at the very center of his or her being. The process takes place in the manner of a deepening spiral: with increasing detachment there comes deeper joy, serenity, and peace, and with

increasing joy, serenity, and peace, the level of detachment grows ever deeper.

Such detachment is one of the ways we become liberated from our various addictions. The other way, we said, is the way of prayer, which opens up when we can call upon some source of power other than our addicted self. Having now been led by the joy of detachment to the center of our being, we are in a position from which we can try to discover this source beyond ourselves.

Perhaps this discovery can be conveniently attempted by reflecting upon a small incident. It happened some years ago when I had the good fortune to spend a week entirely on my own in a cottage high on a Welsh mountainside. Without the noise of radio, or television, or the telephone, the days passed in deep silence. I walked the mountain, gathered blackberries, meditated, prayed and, as it turned out, was not called upon to speak to another human being. Soon after sundown I would go to sleep, and I would awake in time to greet the dawn. During the course of the week, this way of living produced a profound effect upon me: in the absence of those peripheral events which usually draw off so much of our energy, all my energies seemed to become centered deep within me. My mind became quiet and, most obvious of all, my breathing became deeper and more rhythmical. I felt serene and at peace.

At the end of the week I set off walking early in the morning to return home, and as I was walking down the mountainside I met a shepherd on his way up. "Good morning," I said to him as we were passing one another, and he answered also with "Good morning." Then when I was about fifteen yards past him the thought suddenly came to my mind. "What a heavenly smile that shepherd gave me!" I was so filled with gladness by this recognition that I felt impelled to reflect further on the incident. As I did so I realized quite clearly what had happened. I had myself smiled at the shepherd a second or two before greeting him, and his wonderful smile was actually a response to my own.

But here is the crucial point: I had smiled at him before I had formed the intention to do so; my smile had arisen from some point deeper than my conscious self, from some point beyond consciousness. This was in contrast to what generally happens with any social gesture, such as a smile; in it there is almost always a strong element of artificiality, a conscious attempt to create an impression—especially with smiling, when the spontaneous element can sometimes become so reduced as to leave nothing but a hideous grimace.

Somehow or other my week of silence in the mountains had put me in touch with that source of power beyond myself which we must be able to call upon if we are to be cured of our addictions. I had, as it were, discovered or uncovered the center of my being, my heart, though by "heart" I do not mean what the word is often taken to mean nowadays: something sentimental, emotional, romantic. Rather I am using the word in its scriptural sense. For in the Scriptures, "the center of man is not the mind but the heart. The New Testament teaches that the heart is the main organ of psychic and spiritual life, the place in man where God bears witness to himself." The heart "is the center not only of consciousness but of the unconscious, not only of the soul but of the spirit, not only of the spirit but of the body, not only of the comprehensible but of the incomprehensible; in one word, it is the absolute center [of a human being]."[50]

With the aid of this definition of the heart, we can see how it is possible to be still and silent and detached, yet at the same time responsive to whatever calls may be made upon one, whether from a Welsh shepherd or from a demanding committee or from a mentally disturbed adolescent. It is possible because, once we have been brought to the point of the heart, we are standing "at the place in man where God bears witness to himself"; we are praying without ceasing, since to pray means to stand in the presence of God at every moment of our lives.

In the Song of Songs there is a beautiful phrase that neatly expresses this capacity of the heart for turning unceasingly toward the presence of God. The phrase, in English, is, "I sleep; but my heart keeps watch."[51] In the Latin translation it is even neater: *Ego dormio sed vigilat cor meum*—"even when my ego goes to sleep, my heart is still awake to the presence of God." Perhaps we can gloss the phrase further and say that in order for the heart to be awake, in order for our energies to be flowing from "the absolute center," we have to put to sleep all that egotism which wastes our energies on superficial and peripheral activities.

Here, however, an inescapable difficulty confronts us. If prayer must arise from the heart, and the heart is the very center of our being, beyond the scope of the con-

---

50. J. B. Dunlop, *Staretz Amvrosy* (Belmont, Mass., 1972), p. 22.
51. Song of Songs 5:2.

scious mind, then it would seem no more possible to deliberately and consciously to come to the place of the heart than it is to add one cubit to our stature by taking thought. You may as well try to practice delivering a spontaneous speech!

Fortunately we are blessed with a beautiful, classic statement of how this difficulty may be overcome. That statement is found in the book titled *The Way of a Pilgrim,* which was written in the middle of the last century by a Russian who had become a pilgrim.[52] In his book, the author tells us how he became a pilgrim after hearing in church the command in St. Paul's first Letter to the Thessalonians, "Pray without ceasing." Though he had obviously heard the phrase before, on this occasion it touched his heart as never before; and so he went around in search of some holy person who could teach him precisely *how* to fulfill the command.

To cut a long story short, after a number of disappointments he eventually found a holy hermit who taught him the Jesus Prayer. And that prayer provides a way by which one may learn to pray and live from the heart.

Really, the Jesus Prayer is most simple. You just begin by saying over and over again with your lips, "Lord Jesus Christ, Son of God, have mercy on me, a sinner," or some equivalent invocation. After repeating the invocation with your lips many, many times, the prayer begins to move to your mind. With your mind, likewise, you repeat over and over again, "Lord Jesus Christ, Son of God, have mercy on

---

52. R. M. French (tr.), *The Way of a Pilgrim* (London, 1965).

me, a sinner." After a time, so you hope and trust, the prayer will descend from your mind into your heart.

About the manner in which the prayer moves from the lips to the mind and then to the heart, a number of observations may prove helpful. In the first place, one has to recognize that by walking the quiet roads of Russia, the pilgrim was blessed with the ideal way of fulfilling the command, "Pray without ceasing," because when you are walking you can say the invocation aloud without the embarrassment or the distraction that one may feel in a densely populated area. Also, walking is such a rhythmic activity that one's breathing becomes rhythmic, the pattern of the words falls into rhythm with that of one's breathing, and so the whole of one's being starts to become permeated with the power of the prayer. When that happens it is time for the mind to take over. With the taking over by the mind, the prayer becomes intense and concentrated that it is sustained throughout virtually every form of external occupation, whether that be gardening or shopping or cooking dinner.

With the taking over by the mind, the prayer becomes so intense and concentrated that it is sustained throughout virtually every form of external occupation.

But at this point one needs to heed a fundamental warning: there can be no guarantee as to when the prayer will descend from the mind into the heart. With some people the descent takes place after a few days of invocation, while others apparently can wait forty years before the prayer descends from their minds into their hearts.

This difference of timing in no way signifies that some persons are more worthy than others. Worthiness does not come into it; it is entirely a matter of God's grace when he decides to make the move. Some people at this stage fall into the sin of hurry; they try to take the matter out of God's hands and put it into their own minds. They attempt to force the prayer down into their hearts by means of the mind. As a result their second state is worse than their first: instead of their minds being liberated by their heart, it is their heart that is enslaved by their mind. The part has usurped the whole; the creature has usurped the prerogative of the Creator.

By contrast, the person who sticks faithfully to the Jesus Prayer, or indeed to any prayer, eventually discovers that the Creator has detached him not only from the addictions of which he is conscious but has even detached from his heart those very desires beyond his consciousness out of which the addictions arose in the first place. There are no limits to what the Creator can do with those creatures who are ready to stop, be still and silent, to empty themselves, to cease their hurry.

7

Daily Life As a Spiritual Exercise

$\longrightarrow$

THE TITLE OF THIS CHAPTER MAY SEEM ODD AT FIRST SIGHT.
Most of us do not naturally connect spiritual exercise with
daily life. If we think about spiritual exercise at all—and
the term itself seems rather quaint, setting you wondering
how you are supposed to do "spiritual push-ups"—then it
is usually in connection with the long retreats from everyday life that members of religious orders make.

However, the fact that we do naturally react to the term
in such a fashion is a sign that we have been unwittingly
misguided into treating holiness as a matter over which
certain professionals (priests, monks, nuns, etc.) have a
monopoly—as if the command to "be holy as your heavenly Father is holy" were not addressed to all human beings
but only to a select few. And it must be acknowledged that
many of these professionals, in the past, have behaved in
such a way and taught in such a fashion as to give the
impression that holiness is so extraordinary a calling that it

makes extremely complicated demands upon anyone who responds to it.

Sometimes, when one reads books or listens to talks by certain religious professionals, one has the further impression that they have jealously devised for themselves the most complicated series of meditations, difficulties, gradations, temptations, introspections and terminology as a way of placing a great gulf between themselves and any amateurs who may have begun to get ideas. The "amateurs" are then left with the feeling that since an absolutely unbridgeable gulf separates them from the professionals, they must be equally cut off from the Holy One. And so it is impossible for them ever to become holy.

Nothing could be further from the truth. There is no unbridgeable gulf between the Holy One and anyone; in fact, he is closer to us than we are to ourselves. And, as we have already learned, it was in longing for each of us to be holy that he created each one of us. It follows, as the night the day, that holiness is the normal condition of humankind—in the sense that it is the norm; it is what each of us is meant to be. And since we also know that we are meant to earn our living by the sweat of our brows and by bringing up the next generation of human beings, it again follows that our everyday life is the gift by

> **There is no unbridgeable gulf between the Holy One and anyone; in fact, he is closer to us than we are to ourselves.**

means of which we are meant to draw ever nearer to holiness. Our daily life is the matter, so to speak, which we are meant to transform into holiness.

That last sentence, or something very like it, has been enunciated many times over the years—so many times indeed that a reader's eye and mind tend to slide smoothly over it, which is a pity, because, if we read the sentence properly it jolts us awake. It awakens us to the exhilarating truth that every single moment of our daily life, every experience, at whatever time and at whatever place, can serve, and is meant to serve, as spiritual exercise—so long as we, by our attitude, recognize that the experience is meant for that purpose. Every single experience of our daily life is grist for the grindstone of holiness. No experience is wasted.

This truth is exhilarating because if we can accept it as true, then there is no way we can lose. We cannot lose once we realize that everything that happens to us is meant to teach us how to become holy. Then, from every single event in our daily lives, we learn about ourselves and thereby come closer to our true selves; by the same token we come closer to the Holy One, who is even closer to our true selves than we are.

Why then, one may ask, if this truth is so simple, liberating, and exhilarating, do so few people—even religious people—appear to accept it? The answer seems to be that most of us do not especially want to learn; we would rather have comfort than learning. And once we base our lives on comfort (or indeed anything other than holiness, such as ambition), then there is no way that we can win; at any moment our comfort may be disturbed. Being aware of this, we spend all our days in strenuous, uncomfortable efforts to protect our comfort!

Caught in this dilemma, we see clearly that the basic assumption we have made is mistaken. We assumed that life is meant to be smooth; and therefore every jolt, pain, friction, upset, fear, every unexpected twist of the road, comes to be regarded not as life but as an interruption of life; life will begin again once more, we dream, when all these accidents of daily life are past. But, of course, that moment never arrives because the story of daily life is the story of life's accidents or obstacles. The obstacles provide resistance, the principle of reality; precisely because they do not slip smoothly out of the way of our desires and thoughts, obstacles are able to provide us with a foothold in reality.

This realization that resistance keeps us in contact with reality, that obstacles mark the way we are to go, and that every event in daily life can be an occasion for growth has been given different formulations at various times. "Everything is grace," says the dying curé of Ambricourt in Bernanos' novel, *The Diary of a Country Priest.*[53] *"Tout ce qui m'arrive est la volonté de Dieu,"* says another—everything that happens to me is the will of God. Or, as it was beautifully put by the holy man, Abhishiktananda, "The heavenly Jerusalem is not in some dream of the future. It is now. One only needs to open one's eyes."[54]

---

53. Georges Bernanos, *The Diary of a Country Priest* (London, 1937), p. 317.

54. *La Jérusalem heureuse n'est pas dans un rêve d'avenir. C'est maintenant. Il suffit d'ouvrir les yeux. C'est cela que je voudrais faire comprendre désormais si je survis.* Abhishiktananda, in a letter written from his sickbed in North India, Dec. 7, 1973.

Of course the very simplicity of these formulations may cause illusions in us if we are in the habit of imagining that simple truths are easy to make real, to realize. As Tolstoy once said, it is easier to write ten volumes of philosophy than to fulfill one of the commandments.

Take, for instance, those beautifully simple and true words just quoted about the heavenly Jerusalem. Then try to realize them on some occasion when your daily life is not running smoothly. I tried to do so on one occasion when I had lost my briefcase containing the visas and passports for which I had waited for months and without which I could not take up my post in the United States. Mentally I kept reminding myself that the heavenly Jerusalem "is now. One only needs to open one's eyes." For a long time it didn't seem to work at all. However, gradually, as I kept on "opening my eyes," at least I began to get the experience into perspective, and a degree of peace came over me. But the most important part of the experience was that it taught me a great deal about my own condition, about how attached I was to certain plans and what areas of my being were especially rotten and decaying, like old planks in a barn that give way at the least touch of one's foot.

That is the truly exhilarating effect of seeing daily life as spiritual exercise. Every event, every moment is a revelation, albeit usually painful. If we pay attention to our reactions to any demand that is made upon us, we can see, by the way that the fibers of our being react, which parts of ourselves are shaky or rotten. In contrast, we are by the same token given a glimpse of our true self, of our true Center, "the place in man where God bears witness to himself."

How much reactions do reveal, if only we will attend to them, is described for us in the story about Bankei. Bankei was a Zen master. Soon after he died the news of his death was given to the old blind man who used to sit outside the *zendo* (temple) where Bankei had practiced his sitting. The old man said how sad he was to hear of the master's death because Bankei had been a very rare person. The blind man said, "You see, since I am blind, I cannot watch a person's face, so I must judge his character by the sound of his voice. And it is this way. When most people are given the news of another person's good fortune or success, of course they congratulate the fortunate person. But virtually always, beneath the words of gladness, I hear another note, a secret note of envy, envy that it is not they themselves who have been so fortunate. Again, when most people are given the news of some calamity that has befallen another person, of course they express their sorrow toward the afflicted person. But virtually always, beneath the words of condolence, I hear another note, a secret note of pleasure and satisfaction that it is not they themselves upon whom the calamity has fallen. With Bankei, however, it was not so. When he expressed his gladness at another's good fortune, all you heard was gladness. When he expressed his sorrow, all you heard was sorrow."[55]

What a marvelous tribute that is from the blind man to Bankei's purity of heart! Bankei was like a perfectly sound bell, free from flaws; no matter on what part of him was struck by the events of daily life, he always gave off a pure

---

55. P. Reps, *Zen Flesh, Zen Bones* (London, 1971), p. 39.

note, unalloyed with egotistical considerations. And any of us, if we choose, can acquire the same fine and delicate hearing as the blind old man sitting beside the *zendo* by paying attention to the notes that we give off when we are struck by external events.

What happens, for instance, when we hear another person being praised? Does that praise instantly produce within us a note of envy? I say "instantly" because that instant reaction is the moment of truth, which reveals what we are really made of—how far our metal is pure and how far mixed with dross. Within a second or two of hearing the praise, we may well find ourselves no longer listening but speaking, and gravely explaining why the praise offered was not really justified. Objectively speaking, no doubt, our demurral may often be correct; but that is not the point of the exercise. The point of the exercise is to listen without flinching to the note that my metal, the stuff that I am made of, gave off in that first instant, before there was time for me to muffle the note with the tinkling cymbal of my crafty mind. Did I, for an instant, hear a note of envy?

Getting acquainted with your own substance, your own stuff, is a practice in which you have to bear the pain yourself, to stop lying to yourself about yourself.

Each person, of course, has to work on himself. No one else can do it for him. Getting acquainted with your own substance, your own stuff, is a practice in which you have to bear the pain yourself, to stop lying to yourself about yourself. Fortunately, in this matter as in so many others, practice makes perfect; and good habits can be acquired no less than bad ones.

About this practice, however, there is a fundamental observation that needs to be made: if properly carried out it is not in the very least depressing. Of course one is pained at noticing, for example, how reluctantly one reacted to a simple request to go out of one's way on an errand; that reaction uncovered a whole area of laziness in one's substance. It is painful to have noticed an instant of fear at a public meeting when a speaker was acclaimed for mouthing what you knew to be a lie that you should rise to denounce and thereby incur unpopularity; that revealed an area of cowardice within you.

Again, it is painful to notice that one began sweating when giving a homily in the presence of VIPs, though there had never been a trace of sweat when one was giving a homily before a group of ordinary people. The body does not lie; by sweating it bore witness to those fibers of one's being that are corrupted by snobbery. Laziness, cowardice, snobbery: these and many other rotten parts of oneself are laid bare in rapid and seemingly uninterrupted succession by the events of daily life, once the decision has been made to recognize daily life as a spiritual exercise.

In view of the way that the events of daily life disclose such wide areas of impurity in our being, how can one maintain that this practice is not depressing? The answer is twofold. In the first place, once you get your breath back after the shock of discovering your true condition, it is both consoling and bracing to realize that you are being thoroughly cured of a harmful illusion. You begin to delight in the taste of truth: truth tastes better with each illusion that evaporates, and you are less and less addicted to the sweet taste of illusion. As an early Buddhist saying puts it:

If you look for sweetness
Your search will be endless
You will never be satisfied
But if you seek the true taste
You will find what you are looking for.[56]

And just as it is consoling to know that you are slowly but surely acquiring a taste for the truth, it is equally bracing to know precisely the diseased areas of your being that are most in need of healing. If, for instance, it becomes clear to you that certain fibers of your being are corrupted by envy, then there is no better way to heal those fibers than to allow the concentrated light of truth to play upon them continually, to burn away the envious parts and allow room for healthy growth. Admittedly you may still feel slightly shocked at the amount of your stuff that needs transmuting before it becomes holy stuff, but at least you have the consoling knowledge that you are no longer working in the dark.

In the second place, our sense of depression arises from the fact that it is very easy to spotlight the diseased parts of our being and therefore to see them clearly. This in turn leads us to magnify their importance. By contrast, the

---

56. William Duffy, *Sugar Blues* (New York, 1975), p. 218.

healing process that results from spiritual exercise cannot be directly observed. Growth in wholeness is slow and imperceptible; it is the same as with health—it is very easy to put your finger on disease whereas it is impossible to put your finger on health.

Nevertheless, although one cannot directly observe or define health and wholeness, it is not difficult for us to know indirectly, by reflection, when we are growing in wholeness and health. We only need to reflect upon how we perceive the world around us, and our fellow beings in the midst of it. When we are jaundiced in our bodies we tend to perceive the world around us, and our fellow creatures, as negative, threatening and bitter, whereas when our bodies are wholesome and our eyes clear, we perceive our surroundings and our fellows as full of light and joy and sweetness.

The same is true of our spiritual condition. The more joy and light and beauty we perceive in the events of our daily lives, the more we can be assured that, despite any immediate, superficial depression, deep down within us an imperceptible growth in wholeness has all the while been taking place. What you perceive is a pointer to the stuff you are really made of. If you are a pickpocket, what you will perceive in the world around you are pockets. If you are a saint, what you will perceive in the world around you are saints.

We have been given a beautiful illustration of such a process of spiritual growth in the writings of Thomas Merton, the monk. When you read his famous autobiography, *The Seven Storey Mountain,* you cannot help but be struck by the jaundiced attitude toward the world that he took with him into the monastery at Gethsemane in 1941. In those days Merton seems to have been really disgusted with the world in the root sense of the word, that is, "distaste"— everything in daily life seemed to leave a bad taste in his mouth. But during his years in Gethsemane, through learning to treat every event of daily life as spiritual exercise, Merton's whole being was gradually transformed; and so, therefore, was his perception of the world. He left the monastery for the first time in 1948 to accompany another monk into Louisville, and he wrote concerning that journey:

> I met the world and found it no longer so wicked after all. Perhaps the things I resented about the world when I left it were defects of my own that I had projected upon it. Now, on the contrary, everything stirred me with a deep and mute sense of compassion.... I seemed to have lost an eye for merely exterior detail and to have discovered, instead, a deep sense of love and pity for the souls that such details never fully reveal. I went through the city, realizing for the first time in my life how good are all the people in the world and how much value they have in the sight of God.[57]

With these words Merton confirms the ancient spiritual maxim that the holier a person is, the less inclined he or she is to judge other people.

So far in this chapter we have been trying to ground ourselves in the attitude whereby the events of daily life are seen as occasions for spiritual exercise, and we have been trying to realize how exhilarating it can be to adopt such an

---

57. E. Rice, *The Man in the Sycamore Tree* (New York, 1972), p. 66.

attitude. At the same time we must acknowledge that it takes time to become grounded in the habit of regarding everyday events as full of spiritual significance. The trouble is that while certain areas of experience seem very easily to take on a spiritual glow, others seem to be completely insignificant.

To give a very obvious example: kneeling in a church or a temple quickly gives one such a glow, whereas getting caught in a rainstorm or cleaning one's private parts are occasions that do not seem easy to turn into spiritual exercises. And yet it is precisely those experiences which at first sight resist spiritual transformation that have to be treasured. If we throw them aside as though they were rubbish, as though they had nothing to do with us, placing a barrier between them and ourselves, we are actually setting up a barrier *within* ourselves, and so destroying our wholeness. The point has been put very forcefully by K. B. Hathaway:

> I am shocked by the ignorance and wastefulness with which persons who should know better throw away the things they do not like. They throw away experiences, people, marriages, situations, all sorts of things, because they do not like them. If you throw away a thing, it is gone. Where you had something, you have nothing. Your

We must acknowledge that it takes time to become grounded in the habit of regarding everyday events as full of spiritual significance.

> hands are empty; they have nothing to work on. Whereas
> almost all those things which get thrown away are capa-
> ble of being worked over.... But most human beings never
> remember at all that in almost every bad situation there
> is the possibility of a transformation by which the unde-
> sirable may be changed into the desirable.[58]

What is most sad is to see people throwing away what you know to be vital for them as though it were rubbish— their own stuff, in fact. With the increase of mobility throughout the world such jettisoning of what has been handed on to people gets more frequent. A girl of Russian Jewish ancestry, for instance, born in Beverley Hills, will decide that she likes neither the Russian nor the Jewish nor the Beverley Hills parts of her, and so she starts to call herself Morning Star, adopts American Indian dress, and claims to be an adherent of Indian religion. Or a young Catholic man from Belfast is sent to an English public school and afterward changes his name and his accent and never lets on where he came from.

In both these cases, the people concerned have tried to throw away their vital stuff, instead of trying to transform it. But if you are born in Beverley Hills of Russian Jewish stock, then that is the prime matter on which you have to work if you are to become holy. If you are born in Belfast of Catholic stock, then that is the prime matter on which you have to work. Of course the prime matter has to be transformed, just as the alchemists of old had to transmute their base metal into gold, but you have to begin with what

---

58. K. B. Hathaway, *The Little Locksmith* (London, 1944), pp. 12–13.

is given to you. You cannot pick and choose that any more than you can decide to emerge from some womb other than the one from which you did in fact emerge.

In order for the practice of collecting the fragments of yourself scattered throughout your daily life to become spontaneous, one good discipline is the habit of keeping a journal. This means sitting down at the end of each day and quietly and slowly pondering over the day's happenings in order to try to discern what has really been going on within yourself and your neighbors amid those happenings. Sometimes in the tranquility of evening it becomes very clear to you why you behaved in a certain way, and how two or three seemingly unrelated incidents were connected in a pattern of behavior that has not only marked that day, but also characterized your behavior for many years.

The patterns reveal your condition. Sometimes, also, when collecting the fragments, one can see patterns in one's neighbors' behavior, and that knowledge helps one to help them. Occasionally it is even possible dimly to discern the finger of God at work in the seeming chaos of the day, healing the divisions between neighbor and neighbor.

It is amazing what insights are granted to a person who will stick to the discipline of keeping such a journal. Moreover, after a time the insights do not have to wait for the tranquility of evening before being realized, since the habit of reflection becomes so ingrained that a person spontaneously assimilates the meaning of incidents almost as quickly as they occur.

This spontaneous assimilation of the meaning of events in daily life proves especially valuable when one is dealing

with a most grossly neglected yet unfailing source of insights, that is, the dreams that come to us each night. It is said that primitive people are always astonished when they discover how very few modern, westernized people remember and pay heed to their dreams. For them such neglect is tantamount to irresponsibly throwing away the crucial messages that the Holy One is sending to the dreamer, in the deep silence of the night, to guide that person along the path of holiness. And, of course, those primitive people are right; it is the height of ingratitude, folly and prodigality to fail to listen to the word which is delivered in dreams. There occur pivotal moments that turn upon dreams in the traditions of all the world religions, as in the case of Joseph, the son of Jacob, in Genesis; or of Joseph, the carpenter of Nazareth, in St. Matthew's Gospel.

How we also may be visited by healing dreams was evidenced by a dream which once came to me at a time when I was extremely upset with myself, frustrated at the gap between how I wanted to behave and how, in fact, I did behave. I would be resolved, for example, to be calm and dispassionate on some occasion when I knew I was to encounter people whose opinions I considered stupid or wicked. Yet when the occasion came around and I did encounter them, it would not be long before I found myself vehemently denouncing their opinions as not only stupid but also wicked. Again, I would be resolved to exercise the utmost patience toward some person or other whose every mannerism irritated me, only to discover within two minutes of meeting the person that I was behaving like a grumpy bear.

This condition of being severely at odds with myself persisted for a long time—until the night, in fact, when I had a great dream. That night I dreamed a dream from which I awoke the next morning in an immediate state of euphoria. I was already in that euphoric state when I remembered the dream, and I knew instantly what was being said to me through it. The dream was about Joseph, the son of Jacob, whose story is told in the Book of Genesis, or, rather, it was about his coat, for the dream was focused upon his "coat of many colors."[59] Remarkably, and unusually, the dream was in color—and such vivid colors! Moreover, the coat that Joseph was wearing with ease and grace did not have a symmetrical pattern of color but was truly patchwork; and no two patches were alike; they were of so many different shapes and contrasting colors.

As I remembered the dream I simultaneously and effortlessly saw its meaning: I am indeed a patchwork job, made up of bits and pieces from all sorts of different places, not regular or symmetrical, stitched together by seemingly contradictory passions. Yet such a realization is not a cause for despair but for thankfulness that patchwork is the stuff out of which the heavenly Father has made me, just as the coat of many colors that Joseph wore with such grace was a gift from his father.

Most interesting, of course, was the fact that the euphoria did not arise in me after—as a result of—my recalling and understanding the dream. It had already come over me before the recall and understanding. This signified that

---

59. We now know that this traditional phrase is actually a mistranslation of the Hebrew words, but that does not nullify the dream.

some sort of change had first taken place in my substance, in the depths beyond consciousness, beyond the reach of the mind, a change of which the dream itself may just have been a symptom—though a most revealing symptom, obviously.

Needless to say, that dream about the coat of many colors has given me a unique feel for wholeness, for integrity, for not being ashamed of the stuff out of which I am made. No matter how ashamed I may rightly be of the soiled condition into which I have allowed that dazzling coat to fall, I am grateful for the stuff itself. No fragment, therefore, of our daily experience is to be brushed aside as just so much rubbish. Properly attended to, it will reveal unexpected beauty.

No fragment of our daily experience is to be brushed aside as just so much rubbish. Properly attended to, it will reveal unexpected beauty.

As with any truth, however, so with the truth that daily life is meant as spiritual exercise, there is a danger that it will be perverted. And with that particular truth history has demonstrated two frequent perversions. The first allows people to hold that so long as they are daily carrying out pious practices in the station of society where they find themselves, then they need not concern themselves with wider issues about the very order of that society. This attitude is often sanctified by pious hymns that assure us that

> The trivial round, the common task
> Would furnish all we ought to ask—
> Room to deny ourselves, a road
> To bring us daily nearer God.

By the second perversion one divests oneself of responsibility for the order of one's day under the pretext of holy indifference; one drifts through the day claiming each event as a special sign from God, an indication, therefore, that one is doing something much more than drifting.

How difficult it is to avoid the first perversion is evidenced by the fact that for almost 2,000 years every generation of Christians has been tainted by it in some measure. So long as they themselves were behaving "piously" and performing spiritual exercises traditional to their station in society, then they have felt their responsibility to be at an end—even when their position made them beneficiaries of an unholy social system.

I never saw this quite clearly until the day I found myself helping with a renewal course for nuns and observed a young, radical priest questioning the nuns to discover whether they were tainted by this perversion. Many of the nuns served as teachers in extremely expensive boarding schools to which the highly privileged children of rich parents were sent to ensure equally privileged positions for them once they had finished their education. The young priest acknowledged that the nuns were very skilled educational technicians—they taught their pupils so well that they passed their examinations. He also recognized that the nuns were genuinely devout in their pious practices, as well as being cheerful and kind.

But, he asked them, did their responsibility end there? Or were they not also answerable for the position they occupied in society? Were they not abettors and beneficiaries of an unholy social system? Should they not at least consider abandoning their present position within the social system and find one more in accord with the Gospel message?

Not unnaturally, many of the nuns reacted fiercely to his questioning. They felt that the young priest was calling into question their very identity—which, of course, he was, and quite rightly, since questioning our identity is the essential preliminary to renewal. Interestingly enough, some of the nuns who felt this threat to their secure identity most keenly were the younger ones. This was understandable because they had not yet become integrated and centered personally, but were still relying on social props for their identity. Some of the older nuns, in contrast, wholeheartedly agreed with the questions and rather sadly said they now wished these questions had been raised earlier in their lives. In looking back upon their lives in religion, these older nuns realized that it was not in order to spend thirty years shoring up positions of privilege that they had originally followed the Lord's call to renounce home and marriage and children.

The note of sadness on the part of those older nuns, regret that no one had raised this radical question earlier in their lives, told one unmistakably that they felt frustrated in their striving for holiness. They had previously allowed the question of their responsibility to be cut short before it ever touched upon their position in society; and, as a result, there remained an area of themselves that had not been

touched by responsibility and transformed into holy stuff.
It was hardly surprising, therefore, that they felt a lack of
wholeness, a lack of integrity.

What-might-have-been in their lives is splendidly illustrated by the story of a nun who, at a crucial moment in her
life, did face the question of whether she was "in the right
place." (I put the phrase "in the right place" in quotation
marks so as to draw attention to the fact that the phrase rep-
resents the Hebrew formula underpinning the beatitudes.
"Blessed are you when you are poor," for instance, means,
"you are in the right place when you are poor"; "blessed are
you when you are being persecuted" is equivalent to "you
are in the right place when you are being persecuted.")

The nun in question, Mother Teresa, was the head of a
department of her college, Loretto, in Calcutta, when she
decided that she was not now in the right place, even
though she had been very happy in Loretto and was doing
useful work there. She now intended to place herself in the
slums of Calcutta as an unenclosed nun serving the poorest
of the poor.

Inevitably her decision provoked all the usual, sensible
arguments against taking such a step. It was foolish, they
said, for Mother Teresa to abandon her established position
in Loretto, where she was doing such good work (forming
the minds of Indian girls from rich, influential families) in
order to pursue a will-o'-the-wisp notion of helping the
poorest of the poor. In her concern for the poor, they said
(as they always do when faced with the poor!) she should
remember that "rich people also have souls." Fortunately
these arguments, and many similar ones, did not deflect

Mother Teresa from her course, and she went on to become one of the richest sources of holy energy that the twentieth century has known.

What, then, is the seeker after holiness to learn from this example of Mother Teresa? Surely, that there is a loss of integrity if the sanctification of "the trivial round, the common task" is used as an alibi for not assuming responsibility for one's position in society. Most people recognize that there is such a loss of integrity if your position in society is that, say, of a prostitute. No doubt there are many pious prostitutes and some of them may even, in a perverted way, envisage their daily life as a spiritual exercise. Nevertheless it remains a perversion; and in order for a prostitute to grow in integrity and holiness he or she will find it necessary sooner or later to give up his or her position in society in favor of some other.

Many of us, however, fail to see that we are in exactly the same position as the prostitute: we are receiving high salaries in exchange for selling our talents to serve unholy causes. Anyone who serves the armaments system, for instance, needs to question that position constantly. So, obviously, does a soldier, a police officer, a judge, a doctor, a teacher, a scientist. I say "obviously" because it is surely obvious that in the modern world all of them, (scientists, soldiers, judges, et al.) are agents of an establishment, a system, and they need constantly to be asking themselves whether that system they are serving is unholy or not.

We can easily blind ourselves to the obvious, however. I remember that a journalist was once very worried about his daughter's sexual life, but remained unconcerned that he

himself continued to work for the *Daily Blank*. Yet the *Daily Blank* has been remorselessly corrupting the people for generations. To that corruption our journalist friend had blinded himself, out of fear that if he were to see what he was doing he would have to accept responsibility for his position within an unholy system. He would have to give up his job just as promptly as he hoped his daughter would cease her sexual adventures.

Therefore, anyone who takes the call to holiness seriously may well have to abandon his or her present position in society, especially if that position is in the higher ranks. This truth is recognized beyond a shadow of doubt by Western thinkers when they turn their gaze toward a Communist or a Fascist society: to be a functionary in such a society, whether as a Minister or a psychiatrist or a university professor, inevitably results in a loss of integrity and is incompatible with holiness. Yet those same thinkers never seem to recognize that this holds true for functionaries in Western capitalist society. Perhaps it is not altogether impossible for someone seeking holiness to serve as a functionary of Western capitalist society, but the chances are very great that such a functionary will sooner or later have to resign.

Among the rare groups in the West who make a serious effort to undertake only those jobs that are compatible with

> **Anyone who takes the call to holiness seriously may well have to abandon his or her present position in society.**

love of holiness are the pious Orthodox Jews known as
Hasidim. Through their zeal for holiness the Hasidim are
liberated from the idolatry of career. Hasidim never seem to
mind how menial or uncomfortable or how poorly paid
their jobs are so long as those jobs are not incompatible
with their religious calling. And by their example the
Hasidim compel the rest of us to confront seriously the
question: What jobs are the ones most conducive to growth
in holiness?

Virtually the same question was put recently to the
Hindu guru, Baba Hari Dass: What occupation is most
helpful to a person pursuing his *sadhana*? And he gave the
intriguing reply that the best sort of occupation is one in
which you are not dependent on other people. The reply is
intriguing because it coincides with one's experience that
in whatever society throughout the world one may move,
the most balanced and reliable people one meets are crafts-
men—carpenters, blacksmiths, shoemakers, potters—
workers who by virtue of their occupation assume responsibility for their own work and cannot blame other people
for its imperfections.

The reply given by Baba Hari Dass also accords well
with the example given by so many of the holy men in the
traditions of the different world religions. There is Saichi,
for instance, the Shin Buddhist in Japan, who practiced
his *sadhana* while making a type of wooden shoe known
as *geta;* being poor, unable to afford writing paper, he used
to save the wooden shavings from the shoes and inscribe
his devout reflections upon them. It was said of the wood-
en shoes he made that those who wore them found him-

self filled with the very same joy that Saichi found in making them.[60] Then there is the great Sufi mystic, Al-Hallaj, who by trade was a wool-carder; and Gandhi, for whom the spinning wheel stood as an instrument of spiritual exercise.

By citing the Hasidim we have already drawn attention to the importance attached in the Jewish tradition to the kind of work you do: you are shaped by what you do for a living. For that reason the ancient rabbis used to insist that a rabbi should learn some honest craft in order to be able to earn his daily bread. It was no accident, therefore, that Jesus, the rabbi from Nazareth, should have been a carpenter, or that Paul, the rabbi from Tarsus, should have been a leather-worker. Such occupations have another supreme advantage, greatly stressed in the Hasidic tradition, which is that those who follow them are never likely to acquire wealth; and wealth is virtually incompatible with holiness.

Jesus' saying that it is easier for a camel to pass through the eye of a needle than for a wealthy man to enter the kingdom of heaven is only one of a whole chain of similar Jewish sayings. According to the Talmud, for instance, "the son of David will come only when there are no coins left in one's pocket." Or again, "religion is about money: how to give it away." In the Christian tradition this emphasis is less marked, perhaps, but it was a Christian, the poet Gerard Manley Hopkins, who expressed most succinctly why it is so crucial to give money away, to cease being wealthy. He was writing to his friend Robert Bridges, who

---

60. D. T. Suzuki, *Shin Buddhism* (London, 1970), p. 91.

had bemoaned the fact that he himself did not have faith. Hopkins said:

> I have another counsel...I think it will be unexpected. I lay great stress on it. It is to give alms. I daresay indeed you do give alms, still I should say, Give more: I should be bold to say, Give up to the point of sensible inconvenience. *Fieri non potest ut idem sentiant qui aquam et qui vinum bibant:*[61] the difference of mind and being between the man who finds comfort all around him unbroken unless by constraints which are none of his own seeking and the man who is pinched by his own charity is too great for forecasting. It must be felt.... It changes the whole man, if anything can; not his mind only but the will and everything.[62]

Hopkins' words about changing the whole man take the argument back once more to the need to assume responsibility for the whole of one's life, including one's means of livelihood. One can summarize the argument by saying that one is shaped by one's occupation, by the position one occupies in society. If that position is necessary for the functioning of an unholy system, whether of industry or teaching or medicine, then one has to abandon the position for the sake of one's integrity, one's wholeness. You cannot grow in holiness so long as your heart is not whole, so long as it is conniving at injustice. If you are poor, on the other hand, and work for your living, your chances of growing in holiness are far greater.

---

61. Roughly translated: they see different worlds, the ones who drink wine and the ones who drink water.

62. *Letters of G. M. Hopkins to Robert Bridges* (London, 1935), p. 60.

We turn now to the second perversion we mentioned, the one whereby the phrase about daily life as a spiritual exercise is taken to mean that so long as you accept everything that happens as the will of God, then the shape or order of your day is not your responsibility—you can just drift along with events as they occur.

You cannot grow in holiness so long as your heart is not whole, so long as it is conniving at injustice.

Against the background of all the world religions such an attitude is certainly perverted, because all of these religions, without exception, lay great stress upon the need to order one's day, one's week, month, year, and span of years according to a pattern. A Muslim, for example, will pray five times a day: before sunrise, then at midday and mid-afternoon, again immediately after sunset, and finally between the time when twilight is finished and dawn has not yet broken. He will observe Friday of each week as a holy day, he will fast throughout the ninth month of Ramadan, and will observe such festivals as *Id Al-Fitr* and *Id Al-Adha* regularly, at the identical period of each year. A pious Jew will pray seven times a day, observe Sabbath each week, and order his life according to a regular series of festivals. And a very similar pattern holds good for Hindus, Buddhists, Taoists, and Shintoists.

Since the day, the week, the year, the very span of life is marked by such order as the world religions have in common it is much easier, of course, for the followers of these religions to realize that daily life is a spiritual exercise. Especially noticeable is the emphasis which all of them place upon the need to rise for prayer before dawn—indeed the Sikhs say that anyone who fails to do so hardly knows the first thing about holiness. For the early hours of the day are especially propitious for meditation and prayer, above all for the prayer of praise as the creature waits for that great symbol of the Creator's power of renewal, the sun, to shed its light upon all creation.

At the other end of the spectrum, in the darkness of the night, prayer takes on a different mood: the petty incidents which often assume absurd magnitude in the hurry of the day are set into proportion by the dark majesty of the night. The inflated pretensions of worldly men recede before the magnificence of the night sky, and a great wave of compassion for all fragile and needy creatures wells up in the heart of the one who is praying.

Such traditional ordering of the days and seasons as we have quoted here is both unknown and alien to the westernized, industrialized world. That lack is, in fact, what makes it a secular world, a chaos. Anyone brought up in that chaos which is the secular world and who has subsequently turned to follow a traditional pattern will testify that simply by following the pattern, first his perceptions and then his whole sense of himself within creation has been transformed. It takes only a short time to sense the change and to learn to distinguish between secular chaos and sacred order.

Throughout the course of one week, rise before dawn and watch the sun come up over the horizon, and then make sure at the end of the day to watch the sun as it slowly sinks below the horizon. It takes no more than that simple discipline to make you realize why religious teachers have always regarded an ordered day as essential for anyone seeking holiness.

Unfortunately for anyone living in the westernized world with its chaotic lifestyle, that minimum necessary order of rising for prayer before dawn and praying also at night is likely also to be the maximum—at least externally. Even a Muslim, determined and devout, must sometimes lose heart at the dislocation that he experiences when trying to sustain his practice of praying five times a day in the face of industrialized society. I think, for instance, of the occasion when I was asked to intervene and intercede in favor of a Muslim student, new to the West, who had been detained at a petrol station because he had taken out his prayer mat, the hour being appropriate for prayer, and began to make the required prostrations.

Almost immediately, the attendants at the petrol station had phoned the police to say that they had on their hands a lunatic who kept prostrating himself. The police had come along and detained the young man. When my intercession was sought, I did take a certain pleasure in explaining to the police and the attendants that, in the country where their petrol came from, the young man's behavior would be regarded as normal and many of their secular habits would lead to their imprisonment.

An external order for the day, therefore, such as one would always follow in a sacred society, is hardly possible in modern secular society. When people are all still drugged

with sleep at dawn; when they switch on their televisions
and radios as soon as they get up and start drinking coffee,
when the lights are on, the traffic is roaring, and television
and radio continue to boom away throughout the night,
then the sacred thread linking human beings to the order of
creation (the rising and setting of the sun, the waxing and
waning of the moon, the subtle changes in the seasons) gets
more and more frayed until it snaps altogether.

People who live in such a chaos can hardly even con-
ceive of how, for example, a distinction can be made
between the mood of the late afternoon and the mood of
the early evening, a distinction which is perfectly clear to
traditional Indian musicians who would never dream of
playing music appropriate to early evening when it is still
late afternoon. Such delicate appreciation is quite beyond a
society whose members play Mozart's "Night Music" at
eleven in the morning and eat hamburgers at midnight.

Living in such a society, the seeker after holiness finds
the need for order blocked at every turn. Since he or she
is constantly threatened from outside by secular chaos,
therefore, it is all the more essential for him or her to
establish an interior principle which will preserve some
continuing thread of order in life. Happily there is such a
principle, a very simple one, which is capable, slowly but
surely, of producing order in even the most chaotic lives.
This principle is enshrined in a dictum of the fourteenth-
century German mystic, Meister Eckhart, who once said:
"Wisdom [i.e. holiness] consists in doing the next thing
you have to do, doing it with your whole heart, and finding delight in doing it."

It is hard to exaggerate the wisdom, the holiness, contained in that saying. Anyone who practices it—and it is essentially practical—will discover that his life is being shaped and ordered from within in a quiet, undramatic, but unmistakable fashion.

Let me offer an everyday illustration. Suppose that a friend has just sent you a book, on a subject that fascinates you. You are eager to read the book; but sitting on your mantelpiece are three or four prosaic letters that really require a prompt reply. If you follow your fascination and begin reading the book, you find yourself only half enjoying it, because part of you is still stuck on the mantelpiece with the letters. If you still continue to follow your fascination, you leave more and more of yourself behind on that mantelpiece; you are no longer wholehearted, and so your delight in reading the book is far from pure. The longer you go on with it, moreover, the further a certain disorder will penetrate into the day, and from that day into the following day and so on. The logical outcome of events arising from the original disordered decision is, of course, complete chaos.

But most of us manage to bring ourselves up sharp before reaching that logical outcome; we violently wrench ourselves back into some sort of order by hurriedly and carelessly writing the letters which we should have written in the first place—experiencing the truth of the saying that "hurry is a form of violence exercised upon time." Disorder, loss of delight, and violence follow one another in quick succession.

But if, instead, one adheres to Eckhart's dictum to do the next thing, to do it with our whole heart, and to find delight in doing it, then the whole scene changes. To begin with, as soon as one starts to write the replies, one discovers that the letters are not quite so prosaic or boring as one had originally labeled them. This discovery is heartening; consequently it becomes surprisingly easy to put one's whole heart into the writing; and when that happens one finds delight in each detail of the writing, because the proper placing of each detail increases one's awareness of order and the delight that goes with it.

Nine times out of ten one knows perfectly well what is the next thing to be done.

Of course Eckhart's dictum is not a universal panacea, and objection is made to it on the grounds that it ignores the main difficulty that one cannot be sure what is the next thing to be done. But the objection is theoretical rather than practical: nine times out of ten one knows perfectly well what is the next thing to be done. If one does it, then nine-tenths of one's confusion is dispelled, one's mind and heart become clear, so that one is left in no doubt even about the tenth case. In that way the principle of order comes to permeate one's next hour and then the day, the week, the year, as more and more of one's aspirations and tasks begin to fall into place and one's life is no longer a secular chaos but a sacred order.

There is, however, a valid element in the objection mentioned from which one can learn a valuable lesson: just as you can become so attached to your position in the order of society that you fail to respond to God's call to change your position, in exactly the same way you can be so obsessed with maintaining order in your daily life that you fail to hear the voice of God breaking through that order.

Quaint and rather pompous expression was once given to that particular obsession by the Victorian scientist T. H. Huxley. Huxley said that if some higher power were to propose to him an agreement whereby he, Huxley, would be so conditioned as on every occasion in life to see what is true and to will what is good, then he would sign such an agreement. It seems to me that Huxley was asking that he should be turned into a piece of clockwork which would react with mechanical correctness to each event of his daily life. In much the same way, a friend of mine once said that she thought it would be much more sensible if God were to let you know at the beginning of each day what was required of you; and then you could go through the list of demands, item by item, and by the end of the day you would have fulfilled the will of God.

Both my friend and T. H. Huxley were in effect saying that they wanted their lives to be ordered in such a way that no unexpected call would be made upon them of the kind that people make upon one another. They wanted a comforting order rather than the disturbing presence of God. But none of us can grow in holiness except by coming closer to the Holy One and responding to the new and unexpected calls made upon us in an intensely personal relationship. Otherwise we would be behaving like lovers about to meet who are so anxious to get the message of their love for one another correct that they each spend hours preparing lists of the manifold ways that they love the other. Then, when eventually they do come together, they decide that there must be an order in their meeting. So they agree that they will read out one item from their lists in turn. With such an arrangement, of course, they might well fulfill their obligations, but they would hardly grow in any way whatsoever. In the face of the beloved, love letters have to be laid aside in order to taste the joy of the beloved's presence.

That is why God frequently has to break through the order that we have established, if he is to call our attention to his presence, lest we settle into our comfortable grooves and sink in them. And there is always an element of surprise, of amazement, in the moment that God breaks in upon his creation.

Indeed, *Surprised by Joy*[63] is the title of an exhilarating book by C. S. Lewis in which the author describes how he, a confirmed agnostic, was finally struck by joy into belief in Christ—to his utter surprise. That surprise was compounded later in a truly hilarious manner, when he, still a confirmed bachelor, was struck by Joy, and was later led to marrying her. I say the manner of it was hilarious because Lewis had previously never had any intention of marrying until it was discovered that Joy was dying of cancer. She needed to stay in England and the only way for her to secure a residence permit was for some Englishman to marry her. In a moment of what the Russians call *umilenie,* "melting of the heart," Lewis married Joy. Her cancer went

---

63. C. S. Lewis, *Surprised by Joy* (London, 1955).

into remission for three years, and Lewis knew such fun
and delight during those years as he had never imagined.

Diligit Deus datorem hilarem says the Vulgate in trans-
lating St. Paul's words to the Corinthians, "God loves a glad
(hilarem) giver.[64] Perhaps St. Paul's original Greek phrase
should even be translated as "God loves a hilarious giver,"
because in the instant of letting go of what you suppose is
essential to you, there is a moment of ecstasy and you can
hardly stop laughing through relief at realizing that it was
not essential to you after all. Something of that hilarity
sparkled around Lewis when he generously gave up his
agnosticism and his bachelorhood.

Lewis' story makes it more readily understandable that
the Russians have a very special icon of the Mother of
God that they call "The Icon
of Unexpected Joy." So often an
everyday incident, seemingly of little importance, is revealed to con-
tain unexpected joy if only we will
respond to it in a spirit of abandon.

Consider, for instance, what
happened to Bill Holt. When he
was sixty years of age, Bill was one
day walking up a cobbled street in
the town of Todmorden, which lies

> **Every event of
> daily life can serve
> as spiritual
> exercise.**

in the Pennine Hills of northern England. Also on the
street was a rag-and-bone man with his horse and cart; the
horse was skinny and ill cared-for, and the man was treat-

---

64. 2 Corinthians 9:7.

ing it badly. Bill was moved at the sight of the horse and protested to the rag-and-bone man. "What's it got to do with you?" the man answered. "Anyway, if you're that concerned about it, you can have it for five pounds."

Bill, of course, had no need for a horse, but in a spirit of abandon, in a moment of what Russians call *umilenie,* he said, "All right. I'll have it." So he paid five pounds that he could ill afford, for a horse of which he had no need. And it changed his life. He gave the horse a name: Trigger. And once he had fed it on the land around his cottage and the two of them, horse and man, had learned to sleep outdoors together, their bodies warming each other, they set out on pilgrimage together all over Europe. They traveled through France and Italy and Spain, Austria, Germany, and the Netherlands. Most often, when evening came, they would ask a friendly farmer to allow them to stay in the corner of one of his fields; Trigger would lie down and Bill would curl up against his belly.

Already a naturally religious person, though not by temperament orthodox, Bill's religious sense deepened tremendously during his years of pilgrimage with Trigger.[65] And who can doubt that his unexpected joy was all contained within that moment of grace when God called to him through a skinny horse and he responded so hilariously?

Every event of daily life can serve as spiritual exercise. And every being can serve as your guru, your teacher, if only you will attend to it—even a skinny horse.

---

65. William Holt, *Trigger in Europe* (London, 1966).

8

Companions and Community

~

BEGINNERS ON THE WAY OF HOLINESS ALL NEED COMPANIONS AND community. And we are all beginners still, as we especially need reminding when we are nearing the end of a book called *Holiness,* because it is easy for us to imagine that having read or written the book, we are now well on the way. Whereas, in truth, all that has happened is that we have some idea of the general direction in which we are going to stride out and one or two tips about suitable footwear and clothing—also, a few stories meant to keep up our spirits on the march.

This need for companionship and community has to be underlined nowadays, when we are witnessing an upsurge of interest in mystical writings, because the language used by mystics easily leads to misunderstanding. In their attempts to express in words the indescribable intensity of their experiences, mystics have to resort to poetical and paradoxical language that is not to be taken literally. It has been said, for instance, that spiritual life is "a flight of the alone to the Alone," or that "religion is what a person does with his solitude"; and comparable phrases could be picked out of the medieval mystical treatise *The Cloud of Unknowing,* or the works of St. John of the Cross.

But one has always to remember that the author of *The Cloud,* and St. John, and almost all mystical writers, simply assume that the readers whom they are addressing are living in the midst of communities and are nourishing themselves on the common life. Similarly when the great scholastic, Duns Scotus, says, *"persona est ultima solitudo; persona est ens incommunicabilis"*—"the person is final solitude; the person is incommunicable being"—we have to remember that he himself was living as a member of the Franciscan family, within the community of the Church.

Growth in holiness means growing ever more deeply into communion with other persons.

What I think Duns Scotus and the mystics are getting at is what we spoke of earlier in this book: that each one of us has to assume ultimate responsibility for our own life. No one else can do it for us; and in that sense each person is *incommunicabilis*, unique, not reducible to a common denominator that would allow one person to be completely substituted by another. But to be responsible itself implies that there is some other being to whom one is responding, and the highest form of that relationship requires that the other being should not be an inanimate object nor even a dumb animal but a being who is also capable of assuming ultimate responsibility—that is to say, another person. From this it is clear that there is no such being as a separate person; if you are a person you are such in response to other persons, and growth in holiness means, therefore, growing ever more deeply into communion with other persons.

In other words, the need for friendship with other persons which most human beings feel is not, in its roots, a sign of weakness but a sign of health. It is not something to be ashamed of but something to delight in, as one delights in the taste of reality. One has to emphasize this truth precisely because certain religious traditions would have us believe that the need for friendship is a sign of weakness, and that the holier a person becomes, the less that person needs other persons, until finally he or she is completely self-sufficient, like an Olympian god, needing no other.

That such traditions are misguided seems obvious from what we have already said, but it becomes crystal-clear in the light of the Christian doctrine of the Trinity. According to that teaching, ultimate reality is Three-Personed, the perfect union of Father, Son, and Holy Spirit. For the human person, holiness means sharing ever more fully in that divine friendship.

Even without the aid of that theological teaching, most religions have intuited that human beings set upon holiness require both the support and the correction of a community whose members are also set upon holiness. Millions of Buddhists, for instance, repeat to this day the phrase given to them by the Buddha: "I take my refuge in the *sangha*," the *sangha* being the community of those

seeking enlightenment in the footsteps of the Buddha. And
Jewish sentiment on the issue is well put by a medieval
writer, Judah Halevi:

> Community prayer is to be sought for many reasons.
> Firstly, the community does not pray for what is hurt-
> ful to an individual, while the individual sometimes
> prays for something to the hurt of other individuals,
> and these pray for something that hurts him; a prayer,
> however, can be heard only if its object is profitable to
> the world and is in no way hurtful. Moreover, an indi-
> vidual rarely accomplishes his prayer without digres-
> sion of mind and negligence: we are therefore com-
> manded that the individual recite the prayers of a com-
> munity, and if possible in a community of not less than
> ten persons *(minyan),* so that one makes up for the
> digression or negligence of the other, in order that a
> perfect prayer, recited with unalloyed devotion, may be
> made, and its blessing bestowed on the community,
> each individual receiving his portion.[66]

While the Jew finds his portion in the *minyan,* and the
Buddhist takes refuge in the *sangha,* the traditional Hindu
goes for support to the *ashram.* An *ashram* is a place of
peace where seekers after holiness come because in that
place, in that community, it is easier really to believe in the
Holy One. In the presence of the holy community, the seeker begins to feel in his or her bones that the pursuit of holiness is not some eccentric aberration, a sign of weakness,
but the most natural thing for any human being. In the
atmosphere of the *ashram,* each person begins to breathe

---

66. Judah Halevi, *Kuzari* 3:19.

more easily and deeply, to feel the good and positive aspirations within growing stronger, and evil and vain desires fading away almost effortlessly.

I say "almost effortlessly" because one has to admit that there is often stubborn resistance on the part of beginners against acknowledging their need for community. The famous French literary critic, Jacques Rivière, was once asked, for instance, why it was that he had stayed away from the Church and the sacraments for such a long time. His simple reply symbolized the attitude of so many people: "It was because I preferred my aching hunger rather than being fed."

At first sight that may sound an improbable, hardly credible statement: that a highly intelligent person would actually choose to hug his aching hunger in preference to taking his fill of food. But reflecting upon Rivière's admission, we recognize how frequently that happens, as well as the reason for it.

When we sit down at the common table those sitting with us are rightly described as our companions, following the Latin words *con*, meaning "with," and *panis*, meaning "bread"—companions are the people with whom we share bread. The essence of that common meal is that every one of the companions should have a share of the food, the conversation, and the attention. In that way, the joy of each becomes the joy of all since the companions have learned to find joy not only in their own share, but also in every one else's enjoyment of the food, conversation, and attention. A really mature companion at table is capable of listening for long periods to the conversation of the others without

saying anything, while also being able to join in when required or even to take the lead on occasion according to the company's needs.

What Rivière had done for many years was to sit at table and refuse to eat as a way of drawing attention to himself, of securing for himself a monopoly of attention. Occasionally he had even left the room and slammed the door, disturbing his companions and immediately monopolizing their attention. He chose to starve his body and soul in order to feed his egotism. Very adolescent behavior, the reader may think—and justly; but the whole of humanity is riddled with adolescent behavior, which is why there is so little companionship and community, especially on the part of someone living in westernized society, which actually fosters egotism and, therefore, immaturity.

Community demands a high degree of maturity.

This point is worth dwelling on because it has been strikingly illustrated by a Japanese psychiatrist. After working for a number of years in the United States, this man began to ask himself what it was in the behavior of American psychiatrists that made him feel uneasy. Eventually it dawned on him that it was their attitude toward their patients: there was a total lack of tenderness between the psychiatrist and his patient. Indeed, it seemed part of the psychiatrist's very image of himself to be hardboiled. In the Americans' attitudes there was a total lack of what the Japanese call *amaeru*. This is a word that any Japanese child can understand, but which seems beyond the grasp of even highly intelligent Americans. Roughly, it means a proper sense of our dependence on other people.

The more he thought about it, the more clearly the Japanese psychiatrist saw that this impasse arose because the Americans and the Japanese envisage the growth of human beings in almost opposite terms. In the American view, a human child is born in a state of utter dependence on his or her parents, relatives, and society, and grows by becoming less and less dependent on others until, in the end, the child is completely autonomous. As the Japanese psychiatrist observed it, this meant the absence of tenderness, of *amaeru,* which in turn explains the terrifying loneliness that afflicts Americans. The paradigm of this life trajectory, from dependence to total independence, is the clinical and lonely deathbed, in the hospital, that is the fate of almost all Americans.

For the Japanese, by contrast, the human child is born in a state of loneliness, incapable of communication with the rest of humanity. The way out of this loneliness leads by way of tenderness into a proper sense of dependence on others. A foothold for tenderness is already given in the child's physical dependence upon others; and the climax of human growth comes at the very end of life. By that time one should have become more and more integrated into the human family, until one dies in the midst of one's community, gladly acknowledging that one is depending upon others at the end—to carry one's body to the proper place for the funeral rites. Certainly no human being, however autonomous, is able properly to dispose of his or her own body.

Of course there are valid elements in both the American and the Japanese vision of growth toward maturity. Certainly it is true that one has to acquire autonomy as a person so as to be capable of integrating oneself as a free person in the community, whether in marriage, in school, or in work. But if growth in holiness does mean, as we have argued, "growing ever more deeply into communion with other persons," then the Japanese vision merits particular attention—especially on the part of Westerners, whose congenital immaturity is symbolized in Jacques Rivière's admission, "I preferred my aching hunger rather than being fed."

All the same, even if Rivière had, in the usual phrase, "gone to church regularly," there is no guarantee that he would have found what each one of us who is "on the path" needs, because not all communities are true communities. For instance, the early Irish saint Comgall visited a certain monastic community and joined in singing the liturgy. Afterward he told the monks that as he was standing in the choir he was granted a vision in which the members of the community were revealed to be bodies without heads. When the startled monks asked what this could possibly mean, St. Comgall replied that a seeker after holiness who has no *anmchara* is "a body with no head." And his vision had shown that none of the monks had an *anmchara,* i.e., a "soul-friend."

Everyone needs a soul-friend, someone who loves you so much that he or she will never allow you to stray from the path of holiness without both rebuking and encouraging you. A community is no community unless you can find there a soul-friend, for otherwise it is virtually impossible to receive the support and the correction which one looks for in a community. The inestimable service that a soul-friend renders to a friend is two-fold: first, to lay bare any self-deception or lying-to-oneself that the friend may be prone to; second, to lift the friend out of depression by giving him or her heart, which is what the word "encouragement" literally means—giving heart, remembering that the only heart one can give is one's own.

On the face of it, self-deception would seem easy to avoid, for who would be so crazy as to want be self-deceived? After all, most of us think of any person who deceives us as the lowest of the low, a betrayer; so merely our own self-interest should make it easy enough for us to get rid of any deception. The only trouble is that you cannot wipe a table clean with a dirty cloth. And in relationship to our own selves each of us can be described as a dirty cloth—above all in matters of religion, for the whole of history shows that there are two classical areas of self-deception, that is, religion and sex. And when they become confused, when one cannot distinguish between one's religious aspirations and one's sexual drives, then a soul-friend becomes a veritable Godsend.

Indeed, a soul-friend has to be a Godsend, has to be sent by God, because you can hardly advertise for one. And even if you could advertise for one, you, who are in need through confusion, would certainly be too confused to choose a true one. In any case, God will send you a soul-friend, whether you like it or not; and then it is up to you to take the healing medicine she gives you. I say "she" instinctively, remembering that it was a woman whom God sent to me when I was in a state of confusion soon after I began on my *sadhana*.

Like many beginners I had made the mistake of talking too much and writing too much about the vistas that open up when one first gets a glimpse of the path. It is a mistake that I see being made constantly with young people in the West who take up Buddhism or yoga or other religious traditions. They are encouraged to become teachers far too early, before they themselves have been properly and patiently formed. No heed is paid to those golden words with which the third chapter of St. James' epistle opens: "Do not be too eager, brethren, to impart instruction to others; be sure that, if we do, we shall be called to account all the more strictly."[67]

Looking back on those years I feel that I would have been shipwrecked had it not been for Ida Friederike Görres,[68] who showed me what it means to be a soul-friend. An extraordinary combination of feminine intuition and masculine firmness, Ida was able, through her loving eye, to see both my talents and my flaws at a glance; nothing seemed to escape her. With one sentence, or even one word, or sometimes simply by the challenge of her eyes, Ida would pick out the false note in something I had said or written and compel me to pay attention to it until I could hear my own falsity ringing in my ears. Never once did she connive at my self-deceptions.

Above all else, she was severe on flattery. Flattery is regarded almost universally in the modern world as a sign

---

67. James 3:1.

68. She was born in 1901, died in 1971, and is particularly known for her powerful study of St. Thérèse of Lisieux, titled *The Hidden Face*.

of good will, even of friendship. Not so with Ida. She had taken to heart the teaching of St. Thomas Aquinas that flattery is a grievous sin; it can do mortal harm to both the one who receives and the one who dispenses it. There was never so much as a flavor of it in our relationship. And yet, equally important, whenever she saw an aspiration of even the slightest generosity arising within me, no matter how wild and preposterous it might have appeared to most people, Ida would light upon it. She would protect and foster it like a mother nurturing a precious child. From her I learned that a soul-friend is one who combines the firmness and austerity expected of a father with the gentleness and warmth expected of a mother.

> **A soul-friend is one who combines the firmness and austerity expected of a father with the gentleness and warmth expected of a mother.**

A simile comes naturally to mind when thinking of the effect made upon me by Ida. Whenever I left her after one of our meetings, or after reading one of her letters, it was as though I had just been fed a ration of good, wholesome bread, home-ground and home-baked. I felt now, as Elijah did, that I also could "walk in the strength of that food for forty days and forty nights to Horeb, the mountain of God."[69] This was in striking contrast to the feelings I used

69. 1 Kings 19:8.

to have upon leaving some other friends, they who were lavish with their flattery. On those occasions I had the sensation of having been fed a diet of chocolate éclairs, which certainly titillate the palate but do nothing for your constitution and drive any thought of holy Mount Horeb right out of your mind.

Indeed, it is surely significant that the very first thing that Ida did, the first time we met, was to provide me with some rough but nourishing bread. It was black bread, the only kind then available in starving Germany after the Second World War. I say it was significant because religious tradition in general insists that a teacher should share food with her pupil before sharing her teaching. By sharing food with someone we are sharing our life; we are establishing a communion within which the handing on of truth is made possible.

This truth is beautifully illuminated by a word used in the early Christian Church: the word *koinonia.* A Greek word, *koinonia* has its root in *koine,* meaning "common." It was a term to describe the kind of Greek in which the New Testament is written, the language of the common people as opposed to the classical Greek language. Its use by the early Church embodies an exhilarating truth about the human condition, since the word *koinonia* meant both communion and community—it is by the act of communion, by breaking bread together, that community is established. The Christian Church is *koinonia,* is communion, community, Eucharist.

This truth that the human community is one with the breaking of bread is not a monopoly of the Christian

Church, even though the Christian Church has accepted it as the center of its worship. An African people, the Masai, for instance, newly evangelized, spontaneously devised a word for the Eucharist that, in translation, means "food for the heart"; food that is shared quickens the heart.

Consider also the story told by Muhammad Assad of his conversion to Islam. Born in Lwow, of an orthodox Jewish family, he had become a journalist in the Middle East, representing a Viennese newspaper. En route, he had abandoned his religion. One day he was traveling by train from Egypt to the Holy Land, and opposite to him in the carriage was a rank-and-file Arab soldier. At one small station the train stopped and the Arab soldier got out to purchase a small loaf of bread. As soon as he had sat down again in the carriage the young soldier broke the loaf in half and offered a half to the stranger sitting opposite him.

Years later, in the snowy mountains of Iran, that same Jewish journalist was converted to Islam, taking the name Muhammad Assad. And in that moment his mind went back to earlier days, to the gesture of that unknown Arab soldier; and Muhammad Assad realized that in the sharing of that loaf some current of communion had then been released which had come to fruition so many years later in his acceptance of Islam as his community.[70]

"Food Is Heaven" is the title of a poem by the Korean poet, Kim Chi Ha:

---

70. Muhammad Assad, *Road to Mecca* (New York, 1955), pp. 83, 216.

Food is heaven
You can't make it on your own
Food should be shared
Food is heaven.

We all see
The same stars in heaven
How natural that we
All share the same food.

Food is heaven
As we eat
God enters us
Food is heaven.

Oh, food
Should be shared and eaten by all.[71]

To that unambiguous testimony from Korea we can add the testimony from Tibet by Lama Govinda when he describes a visit made to the village of Poo by the holy Phiyang Lama. Lama Govinda tells of how Phiyang Lama went into retreat until he had so centered himself as to have actually become a focus of divine reality:

He had become the very embodiment of Tsé pamé, the Buddha of Infinite Life. His vision had become visible and communicable to all who attended the ritual, which held everybody spellbound and in a state of spiritual elation. The rhythm of mantric incantations and mystic gestures was like the weaving of a magic net, in which the audience was drawn together toward an invisible center. The sense

71. Kin Chi Ha, *The Gold-Crowned Jesus and Other Writings* (Maryknoll, 1978), p. 30.

of participation was heightened when everybody received Tsé pamé's blessings with a few drops of consecrated water and a small *tsé-ril,* a red consecrated pill of sweetened *tsampa,* representing the Wine and Bread of Life. It was the most beautiful eucharistic rite we had ever witnessed, because it was performed by a man who had truly given his own blood and flesh, sacrificed his own personality, in order to make it a vessel of divine forces.[72]

No wonder, therefore, when Jesus came proclaiming the kingdom of heaven, he so frequently likened the kingdom to a feast, to the sharing of a common meal. Nor were his parables about the heavenly kingdom as a common meal simply fanciful literary devices. If the Gospels are anything to go by, Jesus really loved dinner parties with his friends and opponents alike; a great deal of his teaching is recorded as having been given on such occasions.

This is particularly noticeable in the accounts of Jesus' resurrection. In the inexhaustibly rich story of the two disciples on the road to Emmaus we are made to realize how one may walk many a mile with Jesus as one's companion, yet never realize it is he until one recognizes him in the breaking of bread. In the Gospel of John we are told that after the resurrection the disciples, fishing on the sea of Galilee, did not know Jesus until he had grilled some fish for them along with some bread and had said to them, "Come and eat."[73]

The invitation "Come and eat" is one that virtually every human being hears from the lips of a father or mother

---

72. Lama Govinda, *The Way of the White Clouds* (London, 1972), pp. 270–1.

73. John 21:12.

during his early years, and the community that is constituted by those words "Come and eat," the family, is for
most people the community where
they learn to grow into deeper
communion with other persons,
which is the essence of holiness.
"There is no greater grace given to
a man under heaven," said Brother
Giles, the companion of St.
Francis, "than to live at peace with
those amongst whom his life is
set." Because anyone who manages to live at peace in any human
community only does so by dint of
constant spiritual exercise, which
is itself a grace from heaven.

**Anyone who
manages to live at
peace in any human
community only
does so by dint of
constant spiritual
exercise, which is
itself a grace from
heaven.**

The family has been percep-
tively described as an *ecclesiola,* a
"little church." It has also been
described as *schola caritatis*, a "school of love," a phrase
often applied to a monastic community. Both descriptions
are most appropriate because the community of the family
depends for its continued well-being on a whole series of
rituals: the common meals, the commemoration of the dead
members of the family, the solemnization of marriages, and
so on, through which each individual has to learn to stop
"doing his own thing," indulging his own ego, and to
attend to the common good.

For this reason it is most important for any seeker after
holiness to carry out the rituals of the community to which

he belongs with the utmost care and devotion—even the simplest of them. "You can tell the condition of a man's soul," said the Russian thinker Fyodorov, "by the way that he makes the Sign of the Cross." Conversely, by the care and devotion with which he makes the Sign of the Cross, a Christian will bring health and wholeness to his soul. A Buddhist, similarly, advances toward enlightenment by care in the practice of bowing, or a Hindu by performing the gesture *namaste* with proper reverence.

Adolescents on the spiritual path are apt to treat these customs and rites of their community with indifference, as though they are rather childish habits, pretty and decorative but irrelevant to the serious pursuit of truth. Their attitude is far misguided, since communal ceremonies are the most powerful means of taking you out of yourself, of stopping you from wallowing in your own misery, or your own self-satisfaction, or your own obstinacy.

It happens, one day, for instance, that you are feeling out of sorts with yourself and your fellows, thoroughly out of kilter, preoccupied with your own concerns. But you at least acknowledge, however grudgingly, that you are a member of the community and that today is the day when a new member is to be welcomed into the community through the ceremony of baptism. So you are obliged to attend the ceremony. And when you do so a sort of miracle occurs.

As you take part in the ceremony, going through the ritual actions, perhaps somewhat mechanically at first, your world begins to change. The presence of the child being baptized, the devotion of the parents and the joy of the faithful slowly but surely begin to dissolve your ego-

tism and your concern with yourself. Your heart is melt-
ed by the age-old ceremony and you are now open to the
full flow of life, in and out of your heart, toward all
beings and from all beings. And if it should happen that
on the same day you also take part in a wedding ceremony and a funeral, rites that encompass the whole span of
human existence, then you will discover that you have
really been taken out of yourself, gripped by the liturgy
and pointed very firmly toward wholeness and away
from adolescent partiality. It was after one such liturgy
that Lama Govinda wrote:

> Never had I realized more thoroughly the importance of
> ritual in religion (and especially in community worship)
> and the folly of replacing it by preaching and sermoniz-
> ing. Ritual—if performed by those who are qualified by
> spiritual training and sincerity of purpose—appeals both
> to the heart and to the mind, and brings people in direct
> contact with a deeper and richer life than that of the
> intellect, in which individual opinions and dogmas get
> the upper hand.[74]

The truth in Lama Govinda's statement is a convincing
answer to anyone who would lightly set aside any traditional ceremony of his community. Until you have assimi-
lated from the ceremony all the enlightenment it contains,
it is a terrible waste to cast it aside. "Whoever does the
truth comes to the light,"[75] says John the Evangelist, speaking like the true Jew that he was—for it is one of the fundamental convictions of Jewish tradition that deed comes

---

74. *The Way of the White Clouds,* p. 271.
75. John 3:21.

before doctrine, that understanding will come to you if only you carry out faithfully and meticulously the good deeds commanded by tradition. These good deeds, of course, include the rites of the cult; indeed, there is a very real sense in which good deeds are rites of the cult, just as rites of the cult are good deeds.

This Jewish conviction was marvelously vindicated not long ago in the Lithuanian city of Kovno in the case of a Jewish professor. Though he had been an agnostic all his life, the professor began to be more and more troubled by the sad, neglected condition of the Jewish graveyard in the city. Since the holocaust of Jews by the Nazis and the harassment of them by the Soviets, no one had taken care of their graves. So the professor decided to do so.

Whether or not he was aware that tending graves is a *mitzvah,* a traditional good deed, I do not know. In any case, the good man simply acquired spades, sickles, and shears and began the job of making the graveyard worthy of those buried there. At first he was on his own, but as the weeks went by, other Jews joined him in the work, most of them being agnostics like himself. Eventually there were some 200 of them, all doing the true thing. But, most marvelous, virtually all of them began to be observant Jews, their Jewish faith alight in them once more. "Whoever does the truth, comes to the light."[76]

The Jewish professor's story highlights for us another blessing that comes to us when we submit our egos to the traditions of the community. Not only does it dissolve our

---

76. *Jewish Observer,* Feb. 1973. Interview with Prof. German Branover.

egos and open our hearts toward the present community of seekers after holiness and put us in touch with them, it also puts us in touch with all those in the past who have striven for holiness. And once we have been in touch with them, we have forever afterward a touchstone by which to judge the quality of behavior in ourselves and in those around us.

Community also puts us in touch with all those in the past who have striven for holiness.

A touchstone is a fine-grained mineral used for testing the quality of gold and silver alloys, by the color of the streak produced by rubbing them upon it. The Jews who tended the graves of their dead brethren in Kovno thereby put themselves in touch with the holy ones of the Jewish tradition, with Moses and Elijah and the Maccabees; and henceforth they had available, often unconsciously, an infallible test of quality. A touch is a touch, no matter how light it may be, and the mark left by it is indelible.

For instance, it is remarkable for how many people the German resistance leader, Dietrich Bonhoeffer, came to serve as a touchstone even though they hardly "knew" him in the conventional sense of the word. Some of them only met him once; one person tells us that he only saw him for a few seconds in a railway restaurant without knowing who he was and without even speaking to him, but Bonhoeffer left an indelible impression upon him. Since then, Bonhoeffer has been present in his life always as a touchstone by which he can test the quality of what is going on around him.

It so happens that a fine expression of what a blessing it is to belong to such a community of tradition comes from the pen of Bonhoeffer himself. It was written when he was already in a Nazi prison, at a time when he had discovered for himself all over again the need to observe meticulously the church's cycle of prayer, hour by hour, day by day, season by season: "In times like these we learn as never before what it means to possess a past and a spiritual heritage untrammeled by the changes and chances of the present. A spiritual heritage reaching back for centuries is a wonderful support and comfort, in face of all temporary stresses and strains."[77]

Nor is the support and comfort of a spiritual heritage derived simply from touchstones such as Moses or Elijah or—since he himself has now become one—Dietrich Bonhoeffer. These and the other great names are the stars, as it were, in the firmament of holiness, the ones who are now easily seen as "successes." But no less helpful to a beginner is an awareness of all the others, the apparent failures or misfits, because the beginner is borne along on the great wave of their aspiration also toward wholeness and holiness, knowing that he too belongs in their company, and that someday it may be said of him what Thomas Blackburn said of other strugglers in his great poem "Post Mortem":

They shall be new at the roots of the sane trees
After the various drugs to ward off disaster.

---

77. Eberhard Bethge, *Dietrich Bonhoeffer* (London, 1970), p. 832, quoting a letter of August 10, 1944.

They shall drift down like leaves from the high fells
To the boles of the trees where no one is a stranger.
They shall celebrate their union with each other,
Men and women, speechless in life, dumb as the roots
    of trees,
In good, good communion of talk and laughter
And prove they are found now who had lost their ways.
For these are those who in the parish of living
Having no good instrument on which to play,
Still worked hard and with the almost nothing
Of their scant tongue and brain on the great symphony.
The man who barked like a dog shall talk of angels.
The girl so far gone no skill could disinter
Her buried soul, in superb parabolas
Of dance and song celebrate the life in her.
O, there shall be no more desolation or crying any-
    where there.
For the great pianist who strummed on one string
With a broken finger, shall have an infinity of chords
And the stopped poet who could only say "Good
    morning,"
Reap with his tongue a harvest of meaningful words.
They shall be written in the middle of the page
Who were in the margin here,
For withdrawn from the body that held them in close
    siege
    There shall be no more desolation anywhere.[78]

So far in this chapter, the emphasis has been put upon
the need of a beginner to accept the support and nourish-

---

78. *The Tablet,* May 26, 1973.

ment that is provided by companions and community. However, once he does this and stops hugging his adolescent, aching hunger he begins to grow into an integrated, wholesome person who not only derives support from the community but also offers it.

And the sooner this happens, the better—better, also, if the offering takes the form of menial work. A. D. Gordon, one of the leading founders of the *kibbutzim* in Israel, says, "The real foundation of all spiritual labor is the actual work of our hands, not in an economic, but in a moral sense, such work is the basis of truth for all spiritual building."[79] How true an insight Gordon was voicing here is plain as day to anyone who studies the history of monastic communities in the Christian Church: communities flourish when all the members take a share in the menial tasks, and they wither whenever some members feel privileged to be excused from them.

The classic epigram on menial work, as brief as it is final, was coined by the Indian sage Vinoba Bhave. Still reckoning himself a beginner, although he was in his mid-fifties, Vinoba was one day emptying and cleaning the latrine buckets in the Sevāgram *ashram* when an acquaintance of his came upon him. The man was shocked that so learned a man as Vinoba, erudite in the scriptures of many religions and master of many languages, should be engaged upon in a distasteful task. Vinoba, he exclaimed, should rather be traveling around India lecturing and giving the benefit of his learning and wisdom to the people. "But," replied Vinoba, "since I help to fill the latrine buckets, why should I not help to empty them?"

79. H. Weiner, *The Wild Goats of En Geddi* (New York, 1970), pp. 214–15.

There is no more to be said. If such holy men as Gordon, Vinoba, Charles de Foucauld, St. Francis, and St. Benedict all feel the need to do menial work as part of their *sadhana,* then those who avoid it do so at their peril. The work need not be so striking as Vinoba's task of cleaning latrines; it can be washing up or making beds or sweeping floors or cobbling shoes or baking. *"Entre las pucheras anda el Señor,"* said St. Teresa of Avila ("God strolls amidst the pots and pans"), for it was from the kitchen of a Carmelite monastery that there emerged one of the great classics of spiritual teaching, *The Practice of the Presence of God,* the author being a lay brother who worked in the kitchen virtually all of his long life.

From the example of this lay brother, Brother Lawrence, comes the last word to be said here on the need for community. In his early years Brother Lawrence had attempted to live the solitary life as a hermit, but the attempt soon threw him into such a state of spiritual insta-bility and uncertainty that he realized he needed to live in community, in submission to a common way of life. Yet his aspiration toward the solitary life was grounded in truth; he was only mistaken in believing that it could not be real-ized except by adopting a hermit state or vocation; he was correct enough in holding that every lover of the Holy One needs periods with the Holy One alone. There have to be periods, said Brother Lawrence, in which we may "worship him, without thought of anything else."[80]

Just as a human lover needs time alone with her beloved, with no one else present to distract her, no matter how

---

80. *The Practice of the Presence of God,* first published in 1693.

deeply she may love others such as her family and friends, so the lover of the Holy One needs periods of time when she is alone, silent and still, free from all distraction, able to devote the whole of her attention to the Holy One. The fact that she needs such periods alone is no reflection on the community to which she belongs; but on the other hand it would be a sign of waning love for the Holy One if the time she set aside exclusively for him were to be so curtailed on account of other claims as to virtually disappear.

For some people, indeed, the time set aside for devoting all their attention to the Holy One has to increase rather than diminish. They are the ones who enjoy that extremely rare vocation, the calling to be a hermit. Such a one was St. Seraphim of Sarov, in Russia, who was drawn ever deeper into the silence of God, in the silence of the deep Russian forests. For almost thirty years Seraphim lived alone in his hidden hermitage, unceasingly repeating the Jesus Prayer, reading Scripture, working his vegetable garden, and clearing timber, never for a moment depriving God of his loving attention.

By responding to the needs of others, above all through prayer of intercession, we are intimately joined to them, in communion with them, even though we may be separated from them by thousands of miles of land or sea.

Yet, though he was alone, no person was ever less separated from other beings than Seraphim. Through his constant prayers of intercession he was joined ever more intimately to all God's creatures, to the bears that came in friendship to his hut, to the mosquitoes that he gladly allowed to feed upon him, and to the innumerable human beings who were healed by the light and warmth of his prayers.

For what distinguishes a true hermit such as Seraphim from a pseudo-hermit is that what takes the pseudo-hermit into the desert or forest is his own desires, while what takes the true hermit there is the needs of others. By our own desires we are separated from others, even if we sit at table with them. By responding to the needs of others, above all through prayer of intercession, we are intimately joined to them, in communion with them, even though we may be separated from them by thousands of miles of land or sea. Solitude and *koinonia* are not incompatible because, by one of those paradoxes in which spirituality abounds, the principle that unites persons in the most intimate *koinonia* is the unique, incommunicable relationship with God that each person shares with every other person.

9

Suffering: Self-Sacrifice

⁓

It is an old saying about any task you undertake that when you have done ninety-five percent of the work you are halfway there. The truth in this paradoxical saying will be acknowledged by anyone who has ever made a piece of furniture or marched thirty miles at a stretch—it feels as though that last piece of precision work or that last mile takes more out of you than all the rest of your efforts put together. The same pattern seems to be repeated in the journey upon which the Holy One draws us—the nearer we get to the Holy One, the more intense the demands made upon us if our course is to be sustained.

There is a sense of shock when we are struck by the intensity of the demands made upon us at this last stage, because up till now what we, for our part, have been doing has been mainly disciplinary. That is to say, we have acquired the discipline to begin the task, to assume responsibility for our own being, learning how to stop, to be silent and detached, how to use our daily life as a spiritual exercise and take our share in the community.

When a person observes these disciplines steadily, year in and year out, he grows serene and balanced. He appears to an outside observer to be so securely centered that nothing could ever shake him. And then something happens. He is struck by a form of suffering so intense that it shakes the very fibers of his being. To him it feels as though he has no center left—indeed as though he had never had a center; and all his hard-won balance seems to have been shattered.

It is at this stage that the seeker is made to feel a complete beginner once more and to realize the truth of Thomas Merton's dictum that no one can become holy without being plunged into the mystery of suffering, a mystery that is insoluble by analytical reasoning.[81] If you try to solve this mystery by means solely of your reason it is as though you have been swept out of your depth into the sea and are stretching out your legs and kicking with them, trying to get a grip with your feet on something firm. You are left with a terrible sense of impotence.

Obviously anyone who tries to write about suffering must equally be overcome by a sense of impotence. *Terribilis est locus iste,* as they used to chant in the old Latin rite for the dedication of a church, "This is a place of awe. Here is the dwelling of God. Here are the gates of heaven."

Suffering is a place where one instinctively removes one's shoes and shrinks from speaking. Here one grasps immediately the need for the warning given by the late

---

81. T. Merton, *Saints for Now,* ed. C. B. Luce (New York, 1952), p. 253.

Cardinal Archbishop of Paris, Veuillot. On his deathbed, where he was dying of a most painful form of cancer, Cardinal Veuillot said, "Tell the priests not to preach about suffering. We don't know what we are talking about. When I think back now to all those won-derful sermons I preached about suffering!" Not that Cardinal Veuillot had been unacquainted with suffering during his previous life; but compared with what had been revealed to him in this last ill-ness, all his previous knowledge seemed to be nothing.

Suffering is a place where one instinctively removes one's shoes and shrinks from speaking.

In fact, Veuillot's words are themselves an echo of the words spoken on his deathbed by the great medieval theologian, St. Thomas Aquinas. During his last illness St. Thomas was granted a vision of God's glory, after which he said, "Compared with what I have seen, everything that I have written seems to me no more than straw." The resonance between the words of Veuillot and of Thomas is notewor-thy because of what Thomas had earlier written concern-ing the beatitude, "Blessed are they that mourn; they shall be comforted." He says that this beatitude is directed espe-cially toward seekers after knowledge, the reason being that all learning produces an impress upon the mind that the learner experiences as painful. The mind suffers an impress that changes the state of the mind, throwing it off its established balance. Learning is a passion, in the sense conveyed by the Latin root of the word "passion," that is, "suffering." Taking the word in this sense, we know precisely as much as we have suffered, neither more nor less.

The sense experienced by Merton and Veuillot of how impotent our reason is to deal with suffering was deepened for me once by a demand made upon me personally. The demand came through a friend of mine, Mary, who in her own body had known a dreadful amount of pain. Over many months she had to watch her young child undergo even more intense pain for which the innocent child was completely unequipped. One day, in her distress, Mary turned to me, almost accusingly, and asked me if I could make any sense whatsoever of all the suffering that had come upon her, especially upon her child. Miserably I had to confess my impotence to provide an answer. But I did venture to say that at such times there always echoed in my mind the words of St. Paul in his Letter to the Romans: "We know that the whole of creation has been groaning in travail until now...to bring forth the children of God redeemed."[82] And both of us were reminded also of a saying of the prophet Mohammed when one of the early companions was undergoing great agony and groaning loudly. Some of the other companions rebuked him for doing so, but Mohammed intervened, saying, "Let him groan, for groaning also is one of the names of God."[83]

Many months later, Mary told me that though the words of St. Paul and Mohammed had been of some help to

---

82. Romans 8:21–2.
83. Martin Lings, *A Sufi Saint of the 20th Century* (Berkeley, 1973), p. 113.

her at that time, what spoke most nearly to her condition was rather my speechlessness, my complete bewilderment in the face of suffering. In her previous sorrows, according to her, many people had said to her, "Yes, I understand," or, even worse, "I do understand, my dear," as though the person speaking had managed by means of intellectual power or imagination to reach that very same pitch of knowledge to which Mary herself had been brought only through years of deep suffering.

The word Mary used to describe my response, "bewilderment," recalled for me the phrase used by St. Mark in his account of Gethsemane. St. Mark says of Jesus, "He began to be bewildered and distressed...." In the face of suffering, Jesus himself hoped that it might somehow be circumvented, since his heart was "breaking into death."[84]

Even from what little we have so far said about suffering, it is obvious that if all aspects of spiritual endeavor are paradoxical, then this final mystery throws up the most paradoxes of all. One of them is that you are constantly learning, apparently acquiring secure knowledge, and then suddenly it is taken away from you. Consider, for instance, the case of C. S. Lewis, who for two generations has been celebrated as defender of robust, secure Christian faith. During the First World War Lewis had experienced considerable suffering as a young officer in the trenches, where he had been wounded. He published a book in 1940 entitled *The Problem of Pain*, in which he offered some very firm and logical arguments on the subject of pain and suffering.

---

84. Mark 14:32–5.

The book was an enormous success, going through many editions—even though a number of readers found it unconscionably smug, as though the author had the subject taped and well under control. Indeed, one Oxford philosopher described it as "a nasty little book" on account of its claim to secure knowledge.

I think that one of the reasons for Lewis' attitude at this time was the fact that although he was already forty-five years old, he was still a confirmed bachelor and did not know the martyrdom of marriage. The word "martyrdom," i.e. "witness," is used here advisedly, in mind of a marriage custom of the Russian Church. Following that custom, the couple who are being married put martyrs' crowns upon each other's heads as witness that from now on neither of them can live according to their own will: from now on each of them is a martyr, a witness to the mystery of suffering in marriage.

Whether my surmise is true or not, it is still the case that a dozen or so years after publishing *The Problem of Pain,* Lewis' neat, cozy bachelor shell was cracked open by the incomprehensible power of femininity, as we have already pointed out, in the shape of Joy Gresham. In 1960, Joy died, and in his agony Lewis kept a notebook which he subsequently published, entitled *A Grief Observed*.[85] It did not appear under his own name but under a pseudonym, because he could not have borne to have that pitch of grief exposed as his own. The book is one of the most harrowing accounts imaginable of how a

---

85. C. S. Lewis, under the pen name A. Clerk, *A Grief Observed,* (London, 1966).

deep personal loss came to shatter the security of a
famous believer. He who had been full of knockdown
arguments to prove the truth of Christianity and its capacity for solving all problems now wrote:

> If my house has collapsed at one blow, that is because it
> was a house of cards.... If I had really cared, as I
> thought I did, about the sorrows of the world, I should
> not have been overwhelmed when my own sorrow
> came. It has been an imaginary faith playing with
> innocuous counters labeled "Illness," "Pain," 'Death,"
> "Loneliness." I thought I trusted the rope until it mat-
> tered to me whether it would bear me. Now it matters,
> and I find I didn't.[86]

Or again, speaking of God, he writes: "He always knew
that my temple was a house of cards. His only way of making me realize the fact was to knock it down."[87] Lewis goes
on: "*My* idea of God is not a divine idea. [Nor, may I inter-
ject, is mine or the reader's or any other human being's
idea.] It has to be shattered time after time. God shatters it
himself. Could we not almost say that this shattering is one
of the marks of his presence? And only suffering could do
it"[88] (i.e., the shattering). One phrase in particular is memorable in view of what we have said earlier, when Lewis
writes: "Bewilderment and amazement came over me."[89]

Those are the very words used by St. Mark to describe
the agony of Jesus in Gethsemane. But what is equally

---

86. Ibid., p. 43.
87. Ibid., pp. 44, 61.
88. Ibid., p. 76.
89. Ibid., p. 25.

striking is that Lewis goes on to say, now that his previous superficial faith has been shattered by the loss of his wife, he would not wish in any way to have back his wonderfully happy life with her if it also meant that he had to slip back into that previous kind of faith, so full of egotism.[90]

With that statement, yet another paradox of this daunting subject is brought out: often when you have undergone some shattering experience which has forced you either to collapse altogether or else to grow spiritually, you say to yourself, "Well, never in a month of Sundays would I wish that experience upon myself or on anyone else. And yet, now it has happened to me, I wouldn't be deprived of it for anything in the world."

That was the precise theme of one of the most moving series of broadcasts made over BBC radio some years ago by a doctor who was dying of a particularly harrowing disease, of which every inroad into his being he could trace by reason of his medical knowledge. He said that the only way in which he could possibly have been changed from being the superficial, self-satisfied person he used to be was by just such suffering as had come upon him. And he thanked God for the change that had been wrought in him. But, he continued, if he could be restored to his former superficial self with his comfortable living, and from that point be shown the suffering that he had in fact undergone in recent years as the price of his transformation, then he would certainly not have chosen the suffering.

90. Ibid., p. 70.

In other words, the initiative could only have come from someone other than himself. And there, I think, our doctor friend put his finger on the essence of suffering—its essence lies in the fact that initiative is taken out of our own hands. So long as our lives are in our own hands, we will never really give up the very thing we need above all to give up if we are to be changed, whether that thing is our money, our house, our good opinion of ourselves, our good name, our health, or our very life. What we do not want to give up is precisely the thing that it is necessary for us to give up if we are to grow. And we would never do so unless we were thrust into it of necessity by some Other.

> So long as our lives are in our own hands, we will never really give up the very thing we need above all to give up if we are to be changed.

These truths which C. S. Lewis and the doctor had both discovered for themselves may be summed up by saying that Lewis had thought suffering to be a problem, but Joy's death had revealed it to be a mystery. The distinction is fundamental. For a problem is a sort of puzzle, as in mathematics, that is susceptible of solution. It is something you may pick up or put down as *you* choose, something that leaves your own fate unaffected as does a crossword puzzle; once you have solved it, you can walk away from it and stand off from it and look back upon it in detachment. Whereas a mystery is essentially a situation in which your own being is somehow at stake, and in this sense each of our own lives is a mystery.

Our own lives also exhibit another feature of a mystery, which is that we are thrust into life without our own choice. No creature, clearly, has ever been consulted about whether he or she wished to be created or not—we are plunged into the passion, the suffering of life before we know anything. And even when we do come to know a great deal about the universe into which we are plunged, this mystery, far from being solved in the way that a problem is solved, actually deepens, the further our knowledge takes us.

Nevertheless, the fact that suffering is a mystery must not be allowed to serve as an excuse for not trying to discover meaning in it: a mystery is such not because it is unintelligible but because its intelligible content is too great for our reasoning faculty. One of the bravest attempts to bring out at least some of that intelligible content is to be found in a short essay by Teilhard de Chardin entitled "The Meaning and Constructive Value of Suffering."[91] He begins his essay by saying, "Illness, by its very nature, tends to give those who suffer from it the impression that they are no use, or even that they are a burden on the face of the earth. A sick man is almost inevitably bound to feel that, in the main stream of life, he is, by sheer misfortune, set apart from all the endeavor and all the stir; his condition seems to have no sense; in the midst of universal action it seems to doom him to inaction."

---

91. Teilhard de Chardin, "La signification et la valeur constructice de la souffrance" in *Le Trait d'union,* no. 45 (1933), pp. 6–11.

This depressing view, Teilhard says, arises from our failure to recognize that "something is afoot in the universe, some issue is at stake, which cannot be better described than as a process of gestation and birth; the birth of the spiritual reality formed by the souls of men and by the matter which they bear along with them." Our failure to appreciate this arises from our tendency to think of humanity as an artificial bunch of flowers, each flower having been separately chosen to make up the bunch, instead of seeing humanity as some great tree whose leaves and blossoms are not artificially chosen but organically related:

> In a bunch of flowers it would be surprising to find imperfect or sickly blooms, because they have been picked one by one and assembled with art. On a tree, by contrast, which has had to fight the internal hazards of its own growth, and the external hazards of rough weather, the broken branches, the bruised blossoms, and the shriveled, sickly or faded flowers are in their rightful place; they reflect the amount of difficulty which the trunk which bears them has undergone before attaining its growth.... The world is an immense groping, an immense search...it can only progress at the cost of many failures and many casualties. The sufferers, whatever the nature of their suffering, are the reflection of this austere but noble condition. They are not useless and diminished elements. They are merely those who pay the price of universal progress and triumph...it is exactly those who bear in their enfeebled bodies the weight of the moving world who find themselves, by the just dispensation of providence, the most active factors in that very progress which seems to sacrifice and to shatter them.

Who can doubt, after reading those words, that Teilhard de Chardin had glimpsed at least some meaning in some kinds of suffering? Certainly many physically afflicted persons have paid tribute to his essay for the courage it has given them to bear their own afflictions. At the same time Teilhard's noble words are directed very much toward illness and sickness, toward those with "enfeebled bodies." They hardly touch upon the darkest area of all, where the mystery of suffering is discovered to be the mystery of evil. Pain and illness, even loneliness and impotence may be borne, but what about the sting of malice that is the quintessence of evil?

There is a sort of dizziness that overcomes one in the face of malice; it has been expressed with haunting memorability by a man who, after having risked his life in the resistance against Adolf Hitler, was awaiting execution for his part in the plot of July 20, 1944. Klaus Bonhoeffer, the man in question, wrote concerning the evil Gestapo officials who were proposing to interrogate him once again, "I am not afraid of being hanged, but I don't want to see those faces again...so much depravity...I'd rather die than see those faces again."[92]

Significantly, almost the same words as those written by Bonhoeffer had been used ten years earlier by another prisoner, Julia de Beausobre, when she was in the hands of the Soviet secret police. She tells us how she managed to endure the tortures, even doing so with some serenity, but that what strained her to the breaking point, the most difficult suffering, was the confrontation with malice and

92. Bethge, *Dietrich Bonhoeffer,* p. 832.

depravity in her torturers. The mere existence of such evil
seemed to argue that, despite her readiness to forgive
them, in the end evil cannot be
eradicated in this world and so is
stronger than love.[93]

**Throughout the
ages human beings
have suffered from
the fear that this
world is rooted in
evil and injustice.**

Throughout the ages human
beings have suffered from that
very same fear, the fear that this
world is rooted in evil and injustice. And from the beginning, like
Julia de Beausobre, they have realized that against that fearful
thought there are no convincing
arguments. Conviction is beyond
argument and can only arise
through the presence, beyond argument, of the Holy One
in the midst of evil and suffering.

That, at least, is the guiding theme of the classical treatment of suffering that is to be found in the story of Job. In
that story we learn how the innocent and just man, Job, at
the instigation of Satan, is stripped of all his possessions and
his children and his health. This stripping is to test whether
Job will now curse God to his face, thus showing that Job's
famed reverence for God was only another name for his
attachment to his possessions, his children, and his health.
His delight was in them and not in the presence of God.

Throughout the first thirty-seven chapters of the Book
of Job, this testing calls forth arguments from Job's com-

---

93. Julia de Beausobre, *The Woman Who Could Not Die* (London,
1938), p. 58.

forters and his wife to show that if an innocent and just man is made to suffer then it cannot be done justly. His comforters, the representatives of traditional, established theology, say that since Job is suffering at God's hands, therefore justly, then Job cannot be innocent; he must be guilty and should acknowledge his guilt. Job's wife, on the other hand, knows that he is innocent, which is to her an argument that since her innocent husband is suffering, there is no justice in the world; and so Job should curse God and die. Job himself, however, will accept neither of these solutions. He refuses to deny his innocence (and the reader knows that it is essential for God's plans that Job should maintain his innocence—otherwise Satan would have prevailed in the test). But he also refuses to abandon his trust in God, although that trust comes near the breaking point on several occasions.

And then, in the thirty-eighth chapter of the book, God himself cuts through all the arguments, speaking to all of us from the heart of the whirlwind, saying, "Who is this that denies Providence with words void of knowledge?" Throughout the following chapters we hear this same refrain as God, in magnificent poetry, evokes the wonders of creation by which Job and his companions and the readers of the book are drawn into the very presence of God.

This is the moment at which Job, by his persistence, by his refusal to deny either God's justice or his own innocence, has made the breakthrough from the traditional idea of God into the very presence of the living God. At this point the tensions between his concept of the innocent sufferer and his concept of the just God cease to plague his mind, because God is

revealed as present in his own heart, which is filled only with joy, with no room left for his own concepts and arguments.

For it is noteworthy that God does not answer the arguments of Job, or of his so-called friends, or of his wife. To have done so would have been to acknowledge that suffering is a problem to be solved and not a mystery within which we can be drawn ever deeper into the presence of God and of one another—and by our very presence assure one another, beyond argument, that it is not evil but love that has the last word. "I know that my Redeemer liveth," is the cry of joy from Job, "and that he shall stand in my place at the last."

Along with the Book of Job there is another treatment of the theme of suffering that has become a classic; that is the argument between the atheist Ivan and the believer Alyosha in Dostoyevsky's great novel, *The Brothers Karamazov*. In the course of the argument Ivan quotes one example of suffering after another in order to justify his turning in the face of the suffering of innocent children and saying to God, "I most respectfully return to you my entrance ticket to your heaven."[94]

One of the stories that Ivan tells Alyosha is especially terrifying. It is about a Russian general, owner of great estates, who was inordinately proud of his hunting dogs. One day a serf-boy on the estate, aged only eight, accidentally hurt the paw of the general's favorite hound. So the general locked the child up. Early the next morning, in the presence of the child's mother, he had the child stripped

---

94. *The Brothers Karamazov,* bk. 5, ch. 4.

naked and ordered the beaters to make the naked child run out into the open. "At him!" yelled the general, and he set the whole pack of hounds on the child. The hounds caught him and tore him to pieces before his mother's eyes.

No matter what may happen in the future, says Ivan, nothing can convince him that there is justice in a world where such sufferings are inflicted upon innocent children. And he challenges Alyosha to put forward some argument that could possibly redeem that sort of suffering. Of course Alyosha cannot find one. Shaken and miserable, the only thing he can do is to turn Ivan's attention, and his own, toward the presence of one "who gave His innocent blood for all and everything." That one, Jesus the Christ, is also shown to be reduced to silence in the face of the accusations made against him in the name of justice. Brought before the chief priests of Israel, and again before Pilate, Jesus remains silent. No words or arguments are of any use in that situation: presence alone is the only thing that has weight, that can carry conviction.

The same is true in Ivan Karamazov's story of the old Grand Inquisitor when he accuses Christ of having brought suffering upon mankind through his gift of freedom:

> When the Inquisitor ceased speaking, he waited some time for his Prisoner to answer him. His silence weighed down upon him. He saw that the Prisoner had listened intently all the time, looking gently in his face and evidently not wishing to reply. The old man longed for him to say something, however bitter and terrible. But the prisoner suddenly approached the old man in silence

and softly kissed him on his bloodless aged lips. That was all his answer.[95]

In Dostoyevsky's novel, again Alyosha is reduced to silence. But in the end, when Ivan the unbeliever is possessed by the devil, it is the presence of Alyosha which saves him: "You drove him away," says Ivan to Alyosha. "He disappeared when you arrived. I love your face, Alyosha. Did you know that I loved your face?"[96] The full significance of this statement can only be appreciated when we remember that the biblical word for face, panim, is also the word used to describe God's presence. Its root lies in the verb "to turn," because it is toward a person's face that we turn to acknowledge his presence. And some persons have such pure faces that their presence turns away the devil and all his arguments.

Considering that they are literary creations, albeit grounded in experience, it is uncanny how the Book of Job and Dostoyevsky's novel prefigure the experience undergone in the concentration camp at Auschwitz during the Second World War by the young Jewish boy Elie Wiesel. One incident especially, recounted by Wiesel in an unforgettable way, seems to reflect so many aspects of the mystery of suffering. It occurred after some breach of the camp rules had taken place and the German guards decided as a punishment to hang a child some ten years or so in age. Standing on the gallows, the child had the sad face of an angel. As the young Wiesel watched the victim being hanged he heard one old

---

95. Ibid., bk. 5, ch. 5.
96. Ibid., bk. 11, ch. 10.

Jew groan, "Where is God? Where is he? Where can he be now?" And a voice within him answered, "Where? Here he is—he has been hanged here, on these gallows."[97]

Throughout all the subsequent years of his life Wiesel has been haunted by that memory and has come to realize that in a sense God and man had exchanged places: "In prison, under torture, man...becomes God. That's the secret: God is imprisoned." God suffers with man, in him; he takes man's place and offers him his own place. There is a perpetual interchange of place between God and man.[98]

God suffers with man, in him; he takes man's place and offers him his own place.

Since it was said at the beginning of this chapter that after you have done ninety-five percent of the work you are halfway there, it is well at this point to pause for a moment and try to pull together some of the strands that we have noticed woven into the mystery of suffering.

In chapter three it was shown that the culminating point of the whole of creation is to be found in self-sacrifice, which means freely to suffer the death of one's self for the sake of others. It is toward the possibility of self-sacrifice that the trajectory of the creation points—from the inanimate creation toward life, from life to consciousness, then on to self-consciousness, and finally to the sacrifice of

97. Elie Wiesel, *Night* (New York, 1960), p. 43.
98. Cf. M. Friedman, *To Deny Our Nothingness* (London, 1967), p. 353.

that very self that has been brought to consciousness. With the appearance of life, the line begins to curve upward, getting steeper all the time, until with the perfect act of self-sacrifice it becomes completely vertical (Diagram A, p. 20).

That is the end, the ultimate. It is literally the climax, for "climax" is a Greek word meaning "ladder"; and the vertical line representing self-sacrifice is the ladder up which human beings may ascend into the transcendent. There is no need for any other ladder; there cannot be another ladder; this is the one, unique, sufficient—none other than the ladder that Jacob beheld in his dream at Bethel. It was set up on the earth, its top reaching to heaven, "and behold, the angels of God were ascending and descending on it."

Before attempting that final ascent we need to draw together all that we human beings have learned in the course of the millennia, the lessons that are imprinted upon our bodies and our minds as a result of the strivings of all those creatures over the long ages. In our very nature we represent those creatures as we recapitulate the story of the whole creation personally by taking total responsibility for the gifts that we have received through them. Only then, when we have drawn together all the lessons and practiced all the disciplines, when we have gathered all our energies into one center of integration, can we be poised at the point where the whole weight of our experience and the meaning of our past life is available to break through into the mystery of suffering and self-sacrifice.

But then, as we have seen, at the point when we seem at last to be poised, completely balanced, in control of our bodies, our senses, our minds, it is precisely at that moment that we are swept off our balance by intense suffering. As we experience that moment it feels as though some Other had struck us from above, with a vertical blow, and left us reeling and gasping. We cannot grasp where we are as we gaze at the sheer, blank, vertical wall of suffering against which we have been thrown. Here we encounter the quintessence of suffering: the smooth flow of our life is unexpectedly blocked; its horizontal trajectory is cut off; this is the end of our lives since they are no longer our own, some Other having irrupted into them from above. To the self this is death.

At first sight it would seem nonsensical to speak of preparing for the Unexpected, since you cannot specify what it is that you are preparing for.

Can this incursion of suffering and death into our lives be anything other than arbitrary and meaningless? Assuredly it need not be arbitrary and meaningless, as we have seen from the examples of people who have found meaning and redemption in suffering and death; but that still leaves us with the task of seeing how that can be so. Put briefly, how can you prepare for the Unexpected?

At first sight it would seem nonsensical to speak of preparing for the Unexpected, since you cannot specify what it is that you are preparing for. Most of the time when we speak of preparing for a future test, we have in mind something like a scholastic examination. In such a case we know beforehand more or less what to expect. We know the subject matter of the examination, the books we have to read for it and the sort of questions that are generally asked. If we prepare for the examination in a disciplined manner and use our minds on the day of the examination then we can be reasonably confident that we shall pass the examination, and certain that we shall not be thrown off balance in the process.

With suffering and death, however, we can have no such confidence. We do not know beforehand even the subject matter of our examination, whether our suffering will be in the form of the malice of enemies or betrayal by friends or a slow death or lonely exile; and what death itself is, no one knows. Nor do we know the questions that we shall be asked, what long-forgotten episodes in our past lives will suddenly be flashed onto the sheer wall before us in seemingly arbitrary connections. If we were to enter an examination room prepared for a paper on French literature, only to discover that it was on nuclear physics, the shock that we would undergo might give us a faint foretaste of the shock that awaits us in that unexpected end-suffering, but it could only be the very faintest.

Does this mean, therefore, that we cannot in any way prepare for the end-suffering? Certainly we have to agree with Thomas Merton that the end-suffering cannot be solved by analytical reasoning. It is beyond the mind, that organ of planning which prepares us for what can be foreseen and anticipated. And yet we are not entirely bereft. We are in fact blessed with an organ whose specific grace it is to respond to the Unexpected. This organ is our heart, upon which the weight of suffering always falls but which is also the source of our joy.

So long as it is not hardened, the human heart has the capacity for embracing suffering as a source of joy. We have already come across C. S. Lewis, who was surprised by joy, and Bill Holt, whose life may well be inscribed beneath the Icon of Unexpected Joy. In both cases the joy welled up within them because their hearts had been prepared for it by the generous way they had responded to the Unexpected, which brings both suffering and joy. Whereas the mind is trained by planning for the expected, trying to secure the future, the heart grows through exercising it in the present, in the risk of love, at this moment when the future is still open, undetermined—beyond the reach of the mind and its plans.

So long as it is not hardened, the human heart has the capacity for embracing suffering as a source of joy.

Because it is the organ for responding to the Unexpected, which brings both suffering and joy, the heart is also capable of ultimately sustaining our balance—even when we are dashed against the vertical wall of end-suffering, when all our other organs, our mind and our senses, are panicking. At that point our mind is telling us that something incomprehensible has happened to us that reveals our whole life to be arbitrary and meaningless. And it would indeed be meaningless, if the last word remained with our mind; our balance would then be completely destroyed because our very principle or center of balance would itself have been utterly lost.

But "the center of man is not the mind, but the heart...the place in man where God bears witness to himself." So even in the moment of end-suffering the heart that has grown throughout the years by responding generously to the Unexpected will make the most momentous, unexpected discovery: what seems to be the end, a sheer, blank, vertical wall of suffering, turns out to be the climax of life, the same ladder Jacob beheld in his dream, "upon which the angels of God were ascending and descending." It is at that point that human beings witness to and are themselves witnesses of the Transcendent—literally, "that which climbs above" the wall.[99]

Clearly there is no possibility of our ascending Jacob's ladder if we have already decided in advance that suffering and joy are mutually exclusive. That decision itself is a most reasonable one, of course, if we rely upon the mind as our ultimate guide, because it is the mind's function to distinguish and define; and, by definition, suffering excludes joy, just as joy excludes suffering. Consequently, those people who rely ultimately upon the mind, among them many psychologists, are bound to conclude that anyone who finds joy in suffering only knows a perverted form of joy. Such a person has to be classified in their categories as neurotic.

But life is more than its definition, and life provides us with many convincing examples of people who find joy in

---

99. From the Latin *trans,* "over," and *scandere,* which means "to climb" and which gives us the word *scala,* "ladder."

suffering yet who could never by any stretch of imagination be described as neurotic. You could never meet a less neurotic person than Mother Teresa, and yet she spent virtually all her days in the midst of the most appalling suffering. She did so by choice.

Or consider the example of the Hasidim who were living in the Warsaw ghetto under Nazi domination during the Second World War. It is the custom of these pious Jews to dance together as they sing in praise of God; and although they knew that it would bring down upon them even more cruelties at the hands of their Gestapo captors, nevertheless they did so on one occasion after another. They danced for joy in the streets of Warsaw, under the noses of their oppressors, finding joy in the midst of the most somber suffering.

Nor is the suffering of Jesus' crucifixion an occasion that one normally and readily associates with joy. But a daring soul from outside conventional Christianity has been bold enough to direct our attention to precisely that element in Jesus' passion. This Japanese man, Makoto Ohashi, says, "I feel very close to the breathing of Jesus during his last moments on the cross. It stirs me more than many lectures and sermons. I picture him killed on the cross, all alone surrounded by scornful and contemptuous people. Very few, I think, appreciate the joy he must have experienced when all were against him."[100]

It is not, of course, that Mother Teresa or the Hasidim or Jesus himself desired suffering for its own sake; to do so

---

100. Tenko-San, *A New Road to Ancient Truth* (London, 1969), pp. 176–7.

would truly be a sign of neurosis. But through the many years that their hearts had been moved by compassion for all the sufferers in this world they had discovered that in this world joy is inseparable from suffering. In heaven, so it is said, there is no room for suffering. But all human experience shows that suffering is a condition of this present world. This can be seen most clearly by a comparison: it is the same as if you know that your beloved is suffocating to death beneath a great pile of dung and brambles and rotting bones. In order to save her, you have no choice but to dig with your bare hands through all that hideous muck. Then, at the last, you have to bite with your teeth through the nauseous smelly string with which she is bound. What joy could any lover ever know who was not prepared to get himself covered with dung and cut with brambles and nauseated upon his palate in order to free his beloved, who is the source of his joy?

To be cut off from suffering is automatically to be cut off from joy.

It would be terrible enough for a lover in that situation if someone were forcibly to prevent him from digging into the heap in search of his beloved. But the very worst thing that could happen would be if he himself proved unworthy—if, out of concern to avoid suffering himself, he refused in the end to plunge into the evil heap.

Consequently, if we ask ourselves, "What is the very worst thing that could happen to me in this life?" the answer would have to be the complete opposite of the answer that worldly folk give. The worst thing that could happen to me in this life is that I should always have perfect health, always have interesting work, and plenty of money to buy things and take holidays, and also manage somehow never to be brought into contact with suffering. If that were to happen to me, I should be turned into a monster, something unnatural, incapable of compassion for other creatures.

To be cut off from suffering is automatically to be cut off from joy. And since we are made for joy, we would have failed monstrously to become what we were meant to be if we were cut off from suffering. Whenever we are removed from suffering for any length of time, we can be certain that we are on the wrong path.

Of course there are different forms of suffering. Some of these have minimal redeeming value; they are the forms, for instance, that we bring upon ourselves as a result of our own excesses—the miseries due, say, to indulging in alcohol or frivolous amusement or sexual infidelity. But as we progress along the spectrum of suffering, touching purer and purer forms, just so do the forms of suffering acquire increasing redemptive power, until the fulfillment of redemption when we come to the ultimate form. That ultimate form of suffering is one where a pure, innocent person sacrifices his very self for the sake of others.

It is against the background of such a spectrum of suffering that we catch a glimpse of why, for instance, in ancient Israel so much importance was attached to the spotlessness or purity of the victim intended for sacrifice. In the injunctions for sacrifice laid down in the Torah we are constantly told that the lamb, the ram, the bullock, the red heifer, all victims for sacrifice, must all be "without blemish,"[101] a phrase which is later taken as equivalent to innocence, purity. In what way such victims could serve as a substitute for another's sin is very hard to see on the surface, but there are two angles from which we can see at least a glimmer of the way.

To begin with, we may remember how our reflections on suffering led us to speak of God and man interchanging places (p. 214): in certain situations one can substitute for the other. In other words, there are conditions in which to occupy a place of one's own does not necessarily imply that no other being can occupy it, can take one's place. Second, there is a mode of being that seems to enable persons to move through the barriers of place, to move easily throughout the most resistant places, even through hardened hearts; and that is the mode of innocence, of purity. "Wisdom," we are told by the Scriptures, "is more mobile than any motion; because of her purity she pervades and penetrates all things."[102]

As to how the innocent can redeem the guilty by taking his place, we cannot claim to see more than a glimmer. That it happens is, however, the clear declaration of Scripture. In St. Paul's Letter to the Philippians he declares that God took the place of a slave, so utterly as to suffer the death of a slave on the cross.[103] In so doing he redeemed all creation—not by means of anything external, says St. Peter,

---

101. See the injunctions in Exodus, Leviticus, and Numbers.
102. Wisdom 7:24.
103. Philippians 2:4–9.

such as silver and gold, but by his very life, with his own innocent and pure blood.[104]

Nor is it only in Scripture that we find examples of the innocent penetrating by purity into places that are barred to others, to the clever and the complicated. In the Russian Church, for instance, there is an ancient tradition of *iurodivi,* or "fools for Christ," people who seem to be able to pass unscathed through the social barriers established by rank, money, nationality, and education. Prince Myshkin in Dostoyevsky's novel *The Idiot* has a touch of such a fool for Christ, and even more so has Alyosha in *The Brothers Karamazov;* he is able to penetrate into both physical and spiritual places that are impassable to the other characters because they are loaded with so much guilt. I have myself encountered such a person as Alyosha. He is still alive.

Graham, this friend of mine, seems not to notice and certainly does not acknowledge barriers of hostility that would daunt the rest of us. He simply passes through them. At one climax of his life this capacity stood him and many others in marvelous stead.

It was in the days when he was a District Officer in a remote part of Africa, and a populous African tribe in his area had broken into rioting and armed rebellion. To quell them by force would have required thousands of troops. Graham, however, simply went among them unarmed, unprotected, stumbling along with his spectacles slipping down his nose and with his bush shorts slipping down over his knees. In village after village he addressed the people,

---

104. 1 Peter 1:18ff.

charmed them, and calmed them, until soon the rioting ceased and they were once more at peace. "I was taken out of myself" was the explanation that Graham later gave to me of why he had been so successful. His own nature scarcely having been touched by worldly calculation, he himself had been touched by the Transcendent and so he was enabled to touch others.

Yet there is a sequel to this story of the saving power of innocence that is equally revealing. Some years after the first rebellion, that same African people again began rioting, and once more my friend Graham set out to walk through the villages and calm them. But this time, although he had by now become a hero among them, Graham met with resistance from the people themselves and he had to abandon his plans. Why was that? Reflecting upon the events subsequently he told me that on this second occasion he had not been "taken out of" himself; on the contrary he had been trying to imitate his own successful behavior during the first rebellion. For a time, at least, he had lost his innocence; he had set up an image of himself as a pacifier, and that image had proved a barrier. He had become self-conscious in the wrong sense, in the sense of the Greek word *hupokrites,* hypocrite, that is, "an actor."

The story of how even a person so candid as Graham may lose his innocence is a warning that even the very best people may slip into the act of calculation, ceasing to be spontaneous and pure. "Innocent," "spontaneous," "pure," "non-calculating," all such words constitute an attempt on our part to describe a condition which most of us remember as having been ours in childhood. Everyone knows instantly what Wordsworth means when he speaks of us in our early days "trailing clouds of glory," when he describes how "Heaven lies about us in our infancy." Yet we also recognize, with Wordsworth, that "shades of the prison-house" begin to close in upon us, until eventually "the vision splendid dies away and fades into the light of common day."[105]

In a sense our whole task in life, after that original loss, is to recover the vision splendid, to break out of the prison-house of the ego into a second childhood, into childhood transfigured. For whereas the innocence of our first childhood is immature, not responsible, unacquainted with sorrow and evil, in our second childhood, innocence is transfigured through responsibility and acquaintance with sorrow and evil. Our spontaneity the second time is not now the superficial spontaneity characteristic of our childish behavior when we simply reacted to events, skin-deep, but that deep spontaneity characteristic of holy people who do not simply react, superficially, but rather respond immediately from the depths of their being, from the heart.

Like Wordsworth, most of us are tempted to despair of ever being able to enter again into that world where we immediately perceive beauty and where we seem effortlessly and spontaneously to do what is good. And, as always, no amount of argument, however skillful, can ever dispel such despair and doubt. Only a real, live example can do so—in the same way that Mother Teresa by her example dispelled doubts about whether holiness is possible in our day and age.

---

105. W. Wordsworth, *Intimations of Immortality from Recollections of Early Childhood.*

For me, the crucial example of spontaneous goodness was given once and for all by a poor Muslim workman whose name I do not even know. It was very early one Sunday morning, not far from Bethlehem. At dawn I had put on my tracksuit and gone for a run through the hills around Beit Jala. On my way back I found myself running along a stony road that was flanked on my left by a high wall that hid me from anyone on the hillside below me. When I came to the end of the high wall I turned sharply, at right angles, in order to descend the steep path to the track along which the local people say Mary and Joseph and the donkey traveled on the way to Bethlehem. As I turned, I encountered four Muslim workmen trudging up the steep path on their way to the quarry above. They were in single file, and so close to me that I almost ran into them. I had just time to shout a greeting to them.

In our second childhood, innocence is transfigured through responsibility and acquaintance with sorrow and evil.

But, to my amazement, by the time I reached the last of the workmen, which can have been no more than four or five seconds after I appeared on his horizon, he had plunged his hand into his lunch bag, taken out a big handful of raisins, and pushed them into my hands with the words, "You are sweating." I was moving so quickly that I could not stop and had to content myself with shouting

"Thank you!" But the word that came unbidden into my mind as I felt the soft skins of the raisins on my sweating palms was "Eucharist"—I felt instantly that the workman and I had shared a moment of eucharist.

As I continued on my way, my amazement at the man's gesture deepened. He had not had the time since I flashed onto his horizon to say deliberately to himself, "Here is an occasion to perform an act of charity," or "Now I must do a *mitzvah.*" His generous deed had been truly immediate, spontaneous. It made me wonder how an obviously poor, uneducated workman could manage to do what in my own experience I have found to be beyond the capacity of the finished products of our seminaries and universities. Humbled, I also realized that none of the skills I had acquired through my own education were worth a straw compared with the gift revealed by that handful of raisins.

It was only afterward that I was given a clue by a Muslim friend to whom I recounted the incident. "*Qalb nazhif,*" he said. "Pure heart. The man must have been faithful over many years in the practice of his faith to have such a pure heart."

I say that my friend gave me a clue by this remark because it made me reflect once again that such gestures can only become spontaneous as a result of constant practice. In this sense, at least, a parallel is provided for us by the sort of skill that some sportsmen acquire. When, for instance, you watch two skillful tennis players playing together you are often amazed at the speed with which they react to one another's shots and the ease with which they perform the most difficult-seeming movements. They do not have time to think; and indeed if they did start trying to think about what their strokes should be they would become self-conscious, their movements would cease to be graceful. They would, in a manner of speaking, have lost their tennis innocence, the purity of their game.

Only at a relatively superficial level, of course, can we draw parallels between athletic skills and spiritual practice, so the parallels should not be pressed too far. Yet we do have St. Paul's warrant for drawing them when he speaks of runners in a race who exercise self-control in all things; but whereas they practice to receive a perishable crown, we who thirst after holiness hope to receive an imperishable one;[106] for "the end crowns the deed," as the Russians say.

And no end in our own day illuminates so profoundly the strivings of the athlete of the spirit as the end that crowned the life of the Polish priest Father Maximilian Kolbe. For in the last act of his life, Father Maximilian recapitulated, better than any arguments can, the mystery of how innocent suffering redeems evil, of how purity may penetrate the thickest of barriers, of how the spiritual man sacrifices himself by exchanging places with the afflicted.

It was at the end of July 1941, in the concentration camp at Auschwitz, that Father Maximilian was called to make that final sacrifice. The German commandant had just picked out ten Poles who were to be starved to death; one of them, Sergeant Francis Gajowniczek, on hearing his own name, broke down at the thought of never again seeing his wife and children. Immediately Father Maximilian stepped

---

106. 1 Corinthians 9:25.

from his place in the ranks of prisoners and quietly said, "I
would like to take the place of Sergeant Gajowniczek."

By that act of self-sacrifice, Father Maximilian not only
put the seal on his own life, but he also gave point to the
strivings of all those beings through whom life had been
transmitted to him over the course of millions of years.
That life he had now sacrificed. To sacrifice means to
"make sacred" or "holy." So when Father Maximilian voluntarily sacrificed his own life by taking the place of a fellow prisoner on the death line, he was "making holy" the
lives of all who had taken part in handing on life to him.
What he did was really the climax, the "en-heading," of all
his previous life; moreover, he could hardly have carried
through that sacrifice had he not previously been "taking
the place" of other people for many years.

It is especially significant that he was already revered by
his fellow prisoners for his practice of literally giving up his
own place in the food line for the sake of others whenever
there was a scarcity of food. That practice of his is so significant because the ability to give up one's place in everyday practical matters, such as food lines or property rights,
is a precondition for developing the spiritual capacity to
take the place of another person in his suffering. We have
already seen how the holy one is "more mobile than any
motion; because of his purity he can pervade and penetrate
all beings" (p. 223) and so, quite literally in the spiritual
sense, stand in their place. With Father Maximilian, that
capacity had become habitual, spontaneous; it was second
nature to him through his practice of prayer. Whenever we
pray on behalf of others, we in some measure put ourselves

in their place, and for many years, for many hours each day he had been in the habit of praying on behalf of others.

Also relevant to our theme is a further aspect of Father Maximilian's story. It is that by the time of his death he had achieved the condition which seems essential if suffering is to be thoroughly redemptive; he had become innocent in the root meaning of the word, "not-harming"—like the sacrificial lamb spoken of in Scripture which is spotless, without blemish, pure.

> **Whenever we pray on behalf of others, we in some measure put ourselves in their place.**

That truth about innocent suffering[107] carries with it a most encouraging corollary for all who hope to be "made holy"; when suffering appears on our horizon it is a sign that we are being considered worthy to serve as sacrificial lambs—pure, so that we can penetrate into the lives of others without harming them, even into the most evil places. It is a sign

---

107. E. Moberly, *Suffering: Innocent and Guilty* (London, 1978). Miss Moberly's book only came to my attention after I had written my own book, but I was delighted to discover that she had dealt in detail with the issue of innocent suffering. For me the most helpful aspect of her book was her insistence that interdependence and vicariousness, far from being optional or additional "extras," are at the very heart of our lives. In the light of that insistence I am emboldened to face up to a truth that I hesitated to articulate: if sacrifice is to be redemptive, vicariously effective, then the victim must be innocent. As a corollary, whenever we see an innocent suffering we can be certain, in spite of our horror at the sight, that in some mysterious way the innocent has been chosen to suffer vicariously, to redeem others.

that we are being drawn toward the climax of our lives
when we may once more recover the "vision splendid"
which we lost along with our innocence; that vision is
already returning to us as we move into our second
childhood, into transfigured innocence, mature spontaneity, when we no longer see beauty through our ignorance of evil, but see beauty through the evil.

Witness to the universality of this truth comes to us from
many different quarters. The Hindu scholar, Dr. V. A.
Devasenapathi, for instance, tells us of the Shaivite's sacred
image, Shiva Nilakantha, the Blue-Throated One, who, as an
old story tells, consumed poison brewed for the destruction
of the universe and bore thereafter in his throat the scar of
the burning. Though he does not equate Shiva with Christ,
Devasenapathi, who is deeply sympathetic to the Gospel,
avows that his own devotion to Nilakantha helps him to
enter some way into the Christian's devotion to the crucified
Christ and "the wound which all my sorrows heals."

Or, as a Shaivite poet sang, "Though I dwelt with the
wicked and the unfree, to me he showed the path of love....
Purifying my mind, he made me Shiva...." And later, "You
made me yours...ate fiery poison, pitying poor souls, so that
even one as worthless as I might taste heavenly food." On
which Devasenapathi comments, "Worship of the Blue-
Throated Shiva demands a readiness on the part of its
adherents to take the sufferings of others upon themselves"; and Nilakantha's devotees live out this faith, often
at great self-sacrifice.[108]

---

108. E. Thacker, "Christ's Passion Seen Through Eastern Eyes,"
The Times (March 18, 1978).

From distant Russia we hear an almost identical theme. There, in the labor camps during the 1930s, Julia de Beausobre heard storytellers telling over and over again a legend about how St. George proved unworthy to be the slayer of Falsehood. He was not worthy, so in the legend, Christ tells him, because his knowledge of evil was still too limited. The camp storyteller, whoever he might be, would always end by saying that only those who have themselves drained every drop of the cup of evil may, after their regeneration, shatter it without fear of bringing woe upon themselves or the world, without danger of spilling the dregs over their fellow men or over Mother Earth.[109]

Which one of us can hear these stories from such distant parts of the world without hearing in them an echo of the words spoken by Jesus in the Garden of Gethsemane? At this point, more than anywhere, we realize the truth of St. Paul's saying that God brought all the agony of creation under Christ, as head, everything in the heavens and everything on earth (p. 28).

The Russian peasants, the Blue-Throated Nilakantha, Father Maximilian Kolbe, all their sacrifices and all other sacrifices are recapitulated by Christ in his agony in the Garden, where he takes the place of all creation. "Let this cup pass from me," he says, "yet not as I will, but as you will." The cup of which he was speaking was the cup into which the Holy Innocent One had drawn all the evils and poisons from all the world and which he was now being asked to drink to the dregs, so that through him no drop of

---

109. Julia de Beausobre, *Creative Suffering* (London, 1940), p. 36.

evil, whether from the past or the present or the future, should remain beyond redemption. Not a drop did he spill, either on his fellow men or upon Mother Earth.

What does all this mean for those of us who have been even faintly touched, no matter how faintly, by "the sadness of not being a saint"? For it has been made clear to us that the climax of the whole creation is self-sacrifice; that is the ultimate in reality; there is nothing beyond it; it is the end. There is the kingdom of heaven. At the same time it appears that the capacity for self-sacrifice which the saints display only develops in those who have become spontaneous, pure, and innocent through joyfully embracing suffering. Most of us, on the other hand, are still very much beginners. We find ourselves neither spontaneous nor pure nor innocent, and we shrink from suffering. We feel to be far from the end, from the ultimate, far from the kingdom of heaven.

And yet here, once again, we stumble across another of those paradoxes with which the spiritual quest is strewn. For if we ask ourselves who, of all the characters in the Gospels, was the one first to recognize the kingdom of heaven on Jesus' own terms, we come up with an unexpected answer. Certainly the professionally holy people, the Jewish scribes and Pharisees, did not recognize his kingdom; nor, clearly, did the Roman authorities and soldiers who in one way or another mocked Jesus' title of king. Nor were his own disciples any more perceptive; from all accounts they wanted their own kind of kingdom where they would be sitting in the judgment seats. Even the most faithful group of all, the women who followed Jesus, do not seem to have grasped what he was offering to them.

In fact, there is only one person who is recorded in the Gospels as accepting the kingdom of heaven on Jesus' own terms, and he was, like Jesus, a condemned criminal nailed to a cross. As he hung there, in his last agony, it was the "good thief" who proclaimed Jesus to be innocent when he said, "Lord, remember me when thou comest into thy kingdom."

The good thief had recognized that even though he himself did not possess that purity by means of which the holy ones can "penetrate and pervade all beings," nevertheless the Holy One himself could penetrate and pervade all beings, including dying criminals such as himself—Jesus was able to come into the place of a good thief and cleanse it and make it spotless for the final consummation. This he did, and that instantly, being "more mobile than all motion."

Perhaps the whole of this book is at the end superfluous, since all anyone need do—so long as he does it with his whole heart— is to say, "Lord, remember me when thou comest into thy kingdom."

Hence, Jesus did not promise the good thief a place in the kingdom tomorrow, or at some future date, but "today"— that is, now, instantly, without any preparation.

Without any preparation the good thief, that total beginner, arrived at the end in an instant. The moment he began he was at the end. So perhaps the whole of this book is at the end superfluous, since all anyone need do—so long as he does it with his whole heart—is to say, "Lord, remember me when thou comest into thy kingdom." Because then he will hear words that will banish every sadness; he will even forget the sadness of not being a saint when he hears the reply from Jesus, "Today thou shalt be with me in paradise."

Epilogue

—

THE CALL OF THE HOLY ONE MAY COME TO US IN ENDLESS different ways, sometimes against our wishes and sometimes, surprisingly, in accordance with them. Many years ago, for instance, I had said to my wife that I would go wherever the Lord might call us. I didn't really care where, except that I hoped he would call us to the Holy Land—though I never imagined that he would do so.

Consequently, the fact that we found ourselves there in 1977, 1980, and from 1981 until 1985 was a surprise and, as it turned out, by no means a pleasant one in every respect. For our years in Jerusalem were to impress on us the truth of Jesus' words to Peter in the classical source for the meaning of "call" that is located at the end of St. John's Gospel. There Jesus says to Peter, "When you were young you went wherever you wished, but when you are old another one will gird you and lead you where you would rather not go."

The surface explanation of Jesus' words is that "another one" (i.e. the Roman governor) was to have Peter bound and led to execution. At a deeper level one might maintain that the "other" in question is God who led Peter to Rome and martyrdom. Even further, Jesus was warning all of us that if we agree to follow him then he will not only lead us to areas of the earth to which we would rather not go, but also to areas of ourselves with which we do not wish to come face to face.

Such, in my own case, was the experience of the four years I spent as Rector of the Ecumenical Institute for Theological Research at Tantur (Jerusalem).

The motif under which I would now choose to place that sojourn in the Holy Land, therefore, is a verse adapted from the Book of Proverbs so as to run: "For the testing of silver—the crucible; for gold—the furnace; for the human heart—Jerusalem."

How appropriate this verse is for anyone living in what the Arabs describe as "that golden bowl full of scorpions" had become obvious to my wife and myself in the course of our first stay at Tantur, in 1977. During those months we could hardly fail to notice what happens to so many people who go to live in the Holy Land. Though they begin with the firm intention to maintain their compassion toward everyone entangled in the tragedy of the Holy Land, the strain of maintaining that compassion toward all people proves to be more than they can bear. Sooner or later they "come down on one side"; that is, on the side either of the Jews or of the Arabs.

For a brief moment their comedown affords them a sense of relief, as happens to us all for an instant when we fall into some sin against which we have long been struggling. But as with sin so in this case; the relief is momentary and the dark consequences more lasting, because having come down on one side justifies us in then demonizing the other side and denying their right to compassion.

So, before setting out for our long stay in the Holy Land, my wife and I established for ourselves various tests that would reveal to us whether we were beginning to lose our compassion for everyone in the land. We agreed that if we were to fail the tests then we would leave Jerusalem and return home, since we would by that token have become a hindrance rather than a help to the peace of that troubled city. One test was as follows. Suppose you hear that a bomb has gone off in a Haifa bus station killing thirteen Jews, seven children among them. Suppose further that the first movement of your heart on hearing the news is such that it might be translated into the words, "Well, of course, I am very sorry for the dead; but what do the Jews expect if they continue to oppress the Arabs?" In that case your heart is ceasing to be a heart of flesh and is turning into a stone.

Or suppose, alternatively, that you hear of an Israeli air attack on a Palestinian refugee camp in Lebanon in which thirteen Arab civilians are killed, and the first movement of your heart is to say, "Well, of course, I am very sorry for the dead, but what do they expect if they continue to live with terrorists?" In that case, also, your heart is ceasing to be a heart of flesh and is turning into a stone.

This test, as well as numerous others which we set ourselves, was to prove particularly demanding by virtue of my office as head of an institute that, according to international law, was in Arab territory, but was several hundred yards inside Israel according to the Jewish leadership. Moreover, since our own community included Jews and Arabs, both Muslim and Christian, as well as scholars of many different nations from every continent and of virtually every Christian denomination, endowed with all the dogmatic tenacity of theologians, I soon realized that my main task was to learn how to live at peace amid constant tension. No less quickly I realized how ill prepared I was, with my limited experience of public office, to serve in such an exposed position. I, who had written about holiness, needed to remind myself of the story told about St. Francis de Sales.

It is told that St. Francis, then a bishop, was one day visiting a convent of nuns where a nun of great austerity and holiness reportedly lived. This report prompted St. Francis to enquire what office in the community this holy nun held. She did not hold any office, the other nuns replied, nor ever had—since she was always so intent upon her devotions, always first into chapel and last to leave, they had felt they could not ask her to do so. "In that case," remarked St. Francis dryly, "let us wait until she has exercised some office in order to discover how holy she is."

In venturing upon this task of living at peace amid numerous tensions, one of the first and, indeed, lasting helps I received came, bizarre though it may seem, from my own book, *Holiness!* I speak of it as bizarre in the same sense that Mary Craig found it strange and slightly hilarious to acknowledge a like experience with her book, *Blessings.* That book recounts Mary's attempts to accept a series of deep sufferings as blessings. Many of her readers assumed that she had now reached a plateau in regard to suffering and was able therefore to take calamities in her

stride. In fact, she herself often falls into abysses of suffering and then has to read her own book, hoping to benefit by
the lessons in *Blessings* which she had earlier tried to pass
on to others.

For my part, alarmed at the multiplicity of calls made
upon me from dawn until bedtime, I turned for help to the
quotation from Meister Eckhart (on p. 160) and tried to
practice it. Almost immediately three things happened. The
first was that I saw quite clearly how impossible it would
be for me to pursue any scholarly work of my own; being
rector was a full-time job and deprived me of any life of my
own. Secondly, and as a consequence of the first effect, I
was completely cured of my addiction to books. Now, as I
gazed upon the wealth of fascinating volumes already in
our institute library, as well as at the new ones regularly
trundled in each week, I could examine them without
attachment, hoping certainly that I might read them some
day while accepting that probably I would never do so.
Thirdly, and most important, these first two liberations disguised as deprivations opened up for me an infinitely rich-
er world, the world of learning presented to me by the fascinating succession of human beings whom I was to meet.
Since I could no longer learn from books, I would take
whoever came to me as my teacher.

Of course there were some people from whom I could
learn very little. Villains, though occasionally amusing,
tend only to confirm what one already knows, that villainy
and vice are boring. But in Jerusalem there is truly a multitude of holy persons; and holy persons are every one of
them sparklingly different from all the others. It was from

them that I decided I could learn how to live at peace in a troubled community. I would give them my utmost attention, watch all aspects of their behavior, listen to everything they said, and, above all, reflect constantly afterward on the secret of their goodness, in the hope of myself coming to share it.

Though the teachings I received are countless, there is one in particular that I will outline here since it applies so directly to living in community; that is, a demonstration of what transparency means.

For over three years, so it seems to me now, I was being prepared through various vicissitudes to learn how precious is the quality of transparency in a human being. The vicissitudes occurred because many of the tensions and subsequent conflicts within the community arose out of the fact that some of us came to the community and came to meetings and discussions—or even to coffee breaks—with hidden agendas. By this I mean that what people said or did was hiding their deeper intentions so that you could not immediately see what they were intent upon. Inevitably this led members of the community to guess at what each other really intended, and this in turn produced a mishmash of suspicion and supposition that occasionally proved inextricable.

Into this situation there came to my rescue an eighty-six-year-old Jesuit of German lineage and Japanese adoption, the Zen master Enomiya Lassalle. He proved to be the answer to my prayers. During his month-long stay with us, I learned to watch him like the proverbial hawk as, day after day, without knowing it or deliberately intending it, he taught me transparency and the freedom that comes from transparency. Whether in the dining room or in his guided meditation sessions, the television room or sitting on a bus, he never ceased to teach me, sometimes gently, sometimes firmly, and often by way of humor.

It was all spontaneous, as in the memorable incident that occurred during his public lecture on "The Way of Zen, the Way of Christ."

The audience seated in our lecture hall numbered some 200, made up from the Christian and Jewish *cognoscenti* of Jerusalem. Some minutes previously I had introduced Father Enomiya to them, and was now ensconced behind the chairman's table set upon our rather over-elevated platform, listening to his introductory remarks. In the course of them he mentioned that for meditation the full lotus position, though desirable, is not absolutely essential. "However," he said, almost as an afterthought, "you should know what it is"; at which this man of eighty-six years calmly walked over to the table where I was seated, jumped on to it, assumed the full lotus position upon it, proceeded to explain the position for a minute or two, and then slipped down from the table, returned to the lectern, and continued with his lecture as if it were all perfectly natural—which it was for him, of course. Only to me, and his sober Jerusalem audience, their eyes popping in astonishment, did it seem outlandish.

What continues to fascinate me about the incident is how clearly it revealed Father Enomiya to be natural, spontaneous, and free. He saw the need to demonstrate the full lotus position; he saw that the table was the most suitable place for the demonstration, so he simply did it. There was no trace of embarrassment in him as he did so nor the slightest trace, either, of playing to the gallery. His was the action of a man who is free because he is transparent, without a hidden agenda or a defensive image.

At the end of his month's stay with us, Father Enomiya's behavior led me to discover a further area of ourselves into which, to adopt Jesus' words to Peter (John 21), we would rather not allow the light to shine. Once more it is the location of a hidden agenda, the deepest hidden, perhaps, of all—where our treasure is....

He and I had to draw up a financial reckoning on the one hand of his travel expenses, fees, etc., and on the other hand of how much he owed us for his stay and that of his companion. The reckoning, on the face of it, was quite complicated, and with certain members of our community might have taken hours. With Father Enomiya it took about five minutes. Our exchanges were totally transparent. Reflecting upon those five minutes subsequently has led me to think that how one deals with money may well be the ultimate test of one's transparency and, therefore, of one's freedom.

Nevertheless, although hidden agendas have to be abandoned if a community is to live at peace, the freedom that ensues is not a freedom to say whatever comes into one's head. So often in communities one hears the phrase "my right to speak" when the person mouthing the phrase has no moral right whatsoever to say anything on the issue at stake. A wealthy person, for example, has no right to lecture a down-and-out on the blessings of poverty.

Moral limits of what one may say were impressed upon me very forcibly over the years by virtue of my having agreed to write a regular "Letter from Jerusalem" for publication in the English weekly, the *Tablet*. Having for decades read thousands of words from the pens of men and women who live far from the daily agony of the Holy Land, whether in London or New York, but who blithely propose their "solution" for the Middle East problem, I resolved never to write a word that might impose any further burden upon the already overburdened inhabitants of the land. This resolution was made easier to carry out because I was acutely aware with every word from my pen that my articles were being scrutinized in the four corners of the world by hawk-eyed characters with conflicting prejudices. The pen, in those circumstances, became an instrument of asceticism.

But the pen is more easily controlled than the tongue— one can erase one's first thoughts on paper, for instance, whereas the word once issued by the tongue passes beyond recall. There is nothing more destructive of community than an unbridled tongue, as I was to discover through my own transgressions. For I still recall vividly three occasions when some unconsidered words of my own threatened the peace of our community. The only consolation I was able to derive in repenting my transgressions lay in the fact that I was thereby driven to plumb anew the significance of certain sentences in St. James' Epistle. I had read those same sentences many times previously but only then, when I was hungry for instruction, did their deep significance come home to me. St. James says, "If anyone makes no mistakes in what he says he is a perfect man.... The tongue is a little member yet it boasts of great things. How great a forest is set ablaze by a small fire. And the tongue is such a fire."

Curiously enough, the practical implications of these observations made by an early Jewish Christian have scarcely been developed at all in the Christian tradition. And I might still have found myself floundering had not providence placed into my hands a classic Jewish treatise which spelled out for me the details of how one should discipline that rebellious member, the tongue. The treatise in question, titled "Guard Your Tongue," is by Reb Yisroel Meir, and the reading of it is enough to put the fear of God into you.

It is said there, for instance, that *loshon hora* (i.e., evil speech) is a worse sin than idolatry, adultery, and murder, and that anyone who constantly indulges in it loses his share in the world to come unless he repents. Moreover, if you are in the company of people who are speaking evil of others, you are obligated to rebuke them. If you do not do so you will be held responsible for their sins.

But of all the unrelenting demands made by the discipline of the tongue, none stood me in such good stead as the one that forbids you to refer in any way to some wrong that another may have done toward you even though it was wrong beyond a doubt.

What made this example so applicable to my own situation was my having discovered by accident certain hurtful remarks *(loshon hora)* which had been made about myself by one or two scholars at a period when they were malcontent. During the following months numerous occasions presented themselves to me, especially in intellectual discussions, when at least on the surface I might quite legitimately have revealed the incompetence of each of them.

However, every time I was tempted to do so there would arise before my eyes the stern portrait of Reb Yisroel displayed on the cover of "Guard Your Tongue." Immediately I would be seized by the fear of God; and so I refrained from saying anything. Silence, I realized, is also an alternative, for "nothing in the whole universe is so like unto God as silence." Very soon even the voice of temptation went silent.

The reward came several months later, almost at the end of the academic year. At dinner one night I felt a wonderfully deep sense of peace and affection and joy flowing from one to another of those of us sharing the same table. Then suddenly I remembered that my table companions constituted the very group that had spoken harshly of me some months earlier. Yet now they were full of affection and warmth. With a shudder, I realized that this wonderful fellowship would have been quite impossible if I had said one such word as I was tempted to say. I made a silent prayer of thanks to God and called a blessing upon Reb Yisroel.

It is worthwhile, I believe, to point out that what came into my mind to help me live at peace, in a moment when I was tempted to break the peace, was not a statement of principle but the image of Reb Yisroel—because it gradually became clear to me over the course of four years that the Holy Spirit brings to birth in you images in the light of which you are enabled to live properly, at peace with yourself and those about you.

At first I did not notice this was happening. Then one day it dawned on me that every time I found myself in a situation of unusual tension there would arise within me some saving image.

The first image that kept appearing before me was something like a capstan. But instead of there being just one rope attached to the capstan there were scores of ropes, and at the end of each of them was somebody pulling with might and main to drag the capstan in their direction. The capstan, I saw, was myself, and the ropes represented my relationship with all the persons and institutions that were trying to drag me on to their side—Arab journalists, American Zionists, Anglicans, Vatican officials, Christian Hebraists, self-proclaimed messiahs, and a multitude of others.

As I gazed at the image of myself as a capstan, I felt a great urge to cut many of the ropes—indeed, all of them, sometimes—for the sake of "my own peace." But then I recognized that you cannot be truly at peace with yourself unless you are working for peace for everyone; and so it would be both wrong and, in the long run, self-defeating for me to break off my relations with any of these contending groups, no matter how fierce the strain they imposed. And as soon as I recognized that to be true I felt greatly strengthened. The capstan became firmer, rather than weakened by the pull of the ropes. Paradoxically, the strength of each pull actually combined now with that of all the others to fix the capstan more immovably into the ground.

After a time, imperceptibly, a different but similar image began to replace that of the capstan. It was the image of a rather weather-beaten tree. Set high on an exposed ridge the tree had many branches, all of which were blown first in one direction and then in another by fierce winds. Sometimes the branches were pressed so close to the ground that it seemed as though the tree itself would be toppled over—on the contrary, however, because the harder the winds blew the deeper the tree sank its roots into the ground, ever deeper into the peace of God.

Then again the image of the tree gave way before a further image, this time of a lake. Once more there were strong winds, this time driving across the lake so that its whole surface was churned up into clashing waves. By now, however, my mind seemed instinctively to know to plunge below the surface of the lake, diving down deeper into the depths to where the water became ever calmer, until eventually I was in a place of complete serenity. I could still sense the churning waves on the surface, it is true, but they were at a distance and did not really disturb the serenity of those vast depths.

This whole process from image to image finally came to a climax beyond images, in a story. It was the story told in the Gospels about the storm on the Sea of Galilee that overtook Jesus and the disciples as they were sailing toward the eastern shore. While Jesus was asleep in the stern of the boat the disciples were thrown into a panic through terror of the storm until eventually they roused Jesus so that he could share their panic. Jesus instead stood up and said to the winds and waves, "Peace." And at once the storm was stilled. For whereas the disciples had allowed the storm outside to get inside them and destroy their inner peace, Jesus had within him that boundless peace which surpasses our understanding, and which stills whatever storm is around us.

The ultimate gift that I received from Jerusalem, therefore, in the midst of all its conflicts, was the gift of peace—not as the world gives, but as Christ gives. For though he promises in this world neither security, nor health, nor wealth, nor long life, nor good reputation, he does both promise and absolutely guarantee that we may have peace at all times and in every place.

Peace to you, good reader.

Index

BOOKS & MEDIA

The Daughters of St. Paul operate book and media centers at the following addresses. Visit, call or write the one nearest you today, or find us on the World Wide Web, www.pauline.org

CALIFORNIA

3908 Sepulveda Blvd, Culver City, CA 90230	310-397-8676
5945 Balboa Avenue, San Diego, CA 92111	858-565-9181
46 Geary Street, San Francisco, CA 94108	415-781-5180

FLORIDA

145 S.W. 107th Avenue, Miami, FL 33174	305-559-6715

HAWAII

1143 Bishop Street, Honolulu, HI 96813	808-521-2731
Neighbor Islands call:	800-259-8463

ILLINOIS

172 North Michigan Avenue, Chicago, IL 60601	312-346-4228

LOUISIANA

4403 Veterans Memorial Blvd, Metairie, LA 70006	504-887-7631

MASSACHUSETTS

885 Providence Hwy, Dedham, MA 02026	781-326-5385

MISSOURI

9804 Watson Road, St. Louis, MO 63126	314-965-3512

NEW JERSEY

561 U.S. Route 1, Wick Plaza, Edison, NJ 08817	732-572-1200

NEW YORK

150 East 52nd Street, New York, NY 10022	212-754-1110
78 Fort Place, Staten Island, NY 10301	718-447-5071

PENNSYLVANIA

9171-A Roosevelt Blvd, Philadelphia, PA 19114	215-676-9494

SOUTH CAROLINA

243 King Street, Charleston, SC 29401	843-577-0175

TENNESSEE

4811 Poplar Avenue, Memphis, TN 38117	901-761-2987

TEXAS

114 Main Plaza, San Antonio, TX 78205	210-224-8101

VIRGINIA

1025 King Street, Alexandria, VA 22314	703-549-3806

CANADA

3022 Dufferin Street, Toronto, ON M6B 3T5	416-781-9131

¡También somos su fuente para libros, videos y música en español!